LIBERAL JUDAISM AND HALAKHAH

edited by

Walter Jacob

A Symposium in honor of Solomon B. Freehof

Rodef Shalom Press
1988

Library of Congress Catalog Card Number
88-092548

ISBN 0929699-00-9

Dedicated to Irene Jacob

in gratitude for thirty good years together

with a prayer for many more

TABLE OF CONTENTS

Preface

Acknowledgements

Introduction

Chapter I - Liberal **Halakhah** and Liturgy
Jakob J. Petuchowski

Chapter II - Reform Responsa: Developing a Theory of Liberal **Halakhah**
Peter J. Haas

Chapter III - Philosopher and **Poseq**: Some Views of Modern Jewish Law
Walter Jacob

Chapter IV - Liberal **Halakhah**: Description, Appreciation, and Critique
Eugene J. Lipman

Chapter V - Liberal **Halakhah**: A Conservative Approach
David Novak

Preface

This symposium was held on May 16 and 17, 1987 at the Rodef Shalom Congregation in order to honor Solomon B. Freehof on the occasion of his 95th birthday. The theme dealt with the subject to which he has devoted the last forty years of his life. We wish him many more years of life and health so that he may continue to contribute to American Jewish studies.

Acknowledgements

We are grateful to the following funds of the congregation which made the symposium possible: The J. Leonard Levy Fund, the Samuel Goldenson Fund, the Solomon B. Freehof Fund, the 125th Anniversary Fund.

Gratitude is likewise expressed to Barbara Baley who worked on the typescript and to others who devoted themselves to the production of this volume.

Introduction

Liberal Judaism emerged from the nineteenth century struggle between tradition and modernity. After half a century of development in German speaking lands it spread to the rest of Western Europe. It also found fertile soil in the United States and Canada; quickly the Reform and then the Conservative movement established themselves and together became the dominant forms of American Jewish religious expression.

Liberal Jewish has been creative; this has shown itself through the evolution of the modern rabbi and synagogue; the reevaluation of the role of the woman; the reformulation of the liturgy and the rethinking of shabbat and festivals. We have welcomed the scientific study of Judaism with its emphasis upon historical and critical insights into the past and produced many of its scholars. After an initial opposition we have joined with Zionism in an effort to renew Jewish spiritual and physical life.

Progress in all of these areas has not been even. Among those which have suffered occasional neglect has been **halakhah**. Although Liberal Judaism concerned itself with **halakhah** from the very beginning, as the debates at the early European and American conferences and synods clearly indicated, practical considerations sometimes led in different directions. We should remember, however that the scholarly founders of Liberal Judaism such as Abraham Geiger, Zacharias Frankel and Leopold Loew dealt with **halakhah.** The American Reform and Conservative movement, heirs to European Liberal Judaism, have demonstrated an increased interest in **halakhah** as shown by debates at conferences and hundreds of lectures and seminars. Books of guidance, numerous responsa, as well as scholarly discussion of religious practice, have met a popular response, yet they have also raised many questions. The nature and basis of Liberal **halakhah** remains unclear. What is the source of its authority? How does the **halakhah** influence other areas of Liberal Judaism? What developments can we expect in this field? This volume does not intend to provide answers to each of these questions but to stimulate further discussion.

Chapter I

Liberal **Halakhah** and Liturgy

Jakob J. Petuchowski

It is fitting that we begin this symposium with a consideration of Liturgy, because Liberal Judaism itself, or Reform Judaism itself, began as a movement for liturgical renewal. Long before Liberal Judaism addressed itself to the revision of such traditional beliefs as those in Revelation and Resurrection, and long before American Reform Judaism abolished the traditional requirements for conversion and divorce, the early Reformers were concerned with the restoration of beauty and dignity to the worship service of the synagogue. Indeed, the editors of the Hamburg Temple prayerbook -- the first prayerbook published for an actual congregation established on the basis of Reform principles -- stated specifically that they did not feel called upon to reform the Jewish religion. (1) Rather was theirs the endeavor to make the service of the synagogue attractive enough to retain -- or to regain -- the devotion of those who, born in the Age of Emancipation, had acquired an aesthetic sense which could no longer tolerate the manner in which Jewish worship in Germany had come to be conducted by the first quarter of the nineteenth century.

Some abbreviation of the liturgy was definitely called for, if only by means of cutting down the number of repetitions in which one and the same prayer tends to be recited in one and the same traditional service. One thinks in this connection of the **Qaddish**, of Psalm 145 (**ashrei**), and of the fourfold recitation of the Prayer of the Seven Benedictions in the course of a Sabbath morning. A sermon in the vernacular was needed to inform the Jewish worshippers, who no longer invariably enjoyed an intensive Jewish education, about the beliefs and teachings of Judaism, and about the meaning of the weekly pericopes of Scripture. So were **some** prayers in the vernacular, - although, with the exception of the Berlin **Reformgemeinde** (Rabbi Samuel Holdheim's congregation), a short-lived attempt by the government of Saxe-Weimar, connived at or even inspired by Rabbi Mendel Hess, to make German the exclusive language of prayer in the synagogue of that duchy, and, later on, the Liberal Jewish Synagogue in London (under Rabbi Israel I. Mattuck's direction), European Liberal and Reform synagogues never adopted prayer in the vernacular to the extent to which the principle of the legitimacy of vernacular prayer was applied in the Reform synagogues of the United States during Reform Judaism's "classical" period -- or even today. And then there was the desire for orderly singing -- rather than speed-reading and shouting -- in the synagogue, which led to the introduction of a choir and of organ accompaniment.

Ideological considerations were to come later, although, already in the Hamburg Temple prayerbooks of 1819 and 1841, prayers for the restoration of the sacrificial cult were reworded to express the hope that our prayers today may be as acceptable to God as were, in ancient days, the sacrifices which our ancestors had brought. Moreover while prayers for the return to Zion and the coming of a personal Messiah did not altogether disappear from the Hamburg liturgy, the prayerbook did not create the impression that the Hamburg Reformers were in any particular hurry to be uprooted from their **Freie-und-Hansestadt**, in order to be transplanted to the Eastern shores of the Mediterranean. (The two volumes of **Die Deutsche Synagoge**, published in 1817 and 1818, and reflecting the services conducted by Israel Jacobson in Berlin, in private homes, did not, unlike the Hamburg prayer book, contain a **musaph** service; but, apart from that, they introduced fewer liturgical changes, motivated by ideological considerations, than the Hamburg Temple prayerbook was to display a few years later.)

It was a layman's movement, that early Reform Judaism, - founded and led by laymen. Of course, some of those laymen - we are thinking particularly of one of the Hamburg Reformers, Meyer Israel Bresselau (1779 - 1839) - may have been far better acquainted with classical rabbinic sources than many Reform rabbis are today; but the fact remains that, while we can date the first Reform worship service in 1810, in the chapel of Israel Jacobson's private boys' school in Seesen, the rabbis did not get into the act until the 1840's, at which time Reform Judaism fully entered the ideological phase of its development. But those concerned laymen, who led Reform Judaism before there was any rabbinic leadership, acted out of a desire to save and to enhance the worship service of the synagogue in the face of the challenges presented by a new age in the history of the Jews. Far from wanting to cause a split in the Jewish community, they thought that their liturgical innovations should be acceptable to **all** Jews. That is why they attempted to justify their liturgical changes with appeals to the traditional sources of the **halakhah**.

We said: "**Halakhah**", rather than "Liberal **Halakhah**", because, whether or not we can speak of a "Liberal **Halakhah**" which may or may not have come into existence **since** those first attempts at liturgical reform, there certainly was no "Liberal **Halakhah**" around in the days of Israel Jacobson and of the Hamburg Reformers. Those Reformers were, in a way and **mutatis mutandis**, in a position similar to that of the first Christians, for whom "Scripture" meant the Hebrew Bible, and who could not yet appeal to a canonized **New Testament**. Thus Paul's proclamation of the abolition of the validity of the **Torah** had to be legitimized by appeals to that very **Torah**. Similarly, the Reformers' deviations from established **halakhic** procedures had to be justified with appeals to the very sources of the **halakhah** which the opponents of Reform regarded as authoritative. And the traditional sources of the Halakhah did, in fact, provide the justifications which the Reformers were seeking. Here is a mere sampling of them:

(1) **Mishnah** Sotah 7:1 (= **B.** Sotah 32a):

The following may be recited in any language: the section concerning the woman suspected of adultery, the confession made at the presentation of the tithe, the **Shema**, the Prayer (of the Eighteen Benedictions), the Grace after Meals, etc." (2)

(2) Maimonides, **Hilkhot Berakhot** 1:6:

All of the benedictions (**berakhot**) may be said in any language, provided that one says them according to their essential character, as ordained by the Sages. And if one has deviated from the formula,as long as one has mentioned the Name of God and His Kingdom, and the subject matter of the benediction, even in the vernacular, one has fulfilled one's obligation. (3)

(3) Maimonides, **Responsum** #256:

Because people do not listen to the prayer leader's repetition of the Eighteen Benedictions, but talk and otherwise behave themselves unsuitable, it is sufficient if the prayer leader alone recites the Eighteen Benedictions, and the congregation listens to him, - (a) because the talking of the people makes a bad impression on the non-Jews who sometimes visit the synagogue, and (b) because the ignorant man, for whose benefit the prayer leader's repetition was instituted in the first place, will see the diversions in which the others are engaging, and he, too, will refrain from listening to the prayer leader. (4)

(4) **Sepher Hasidim**, #588, ed. Margaliot, p. 384:

If someone who does not know Hebrew comes to you, and he is a God-fearing person, or if a woman comes to you, tell them to learn the prayers in the language which they do understand. For prayer only takes place when the heart understands. And if the heart does not know what a man utters with his mouth, of what use is such a prayer to him? Therefore it is better for a man to pray in the language which he does understand (5).

(5) **Sepher Hasidim**, #785, ed. Margaliot, p. 466:

It is better for a man to say his prayer and to recite the **Shema** and its benedictions in a language which he understands than for him to pray in the Holy Tongue, if he does not understand it. (6)

(6) **Shulhan Arukh, Orah Hayyim** 101:4:

A man can pray in whatever language he desires. This applies to prayer offered in a congregation; but an individual should pray only in the Holy Tongue. However, there are those who say that the latter provision applies solely to him who voices his own needs, such as one who prays for the sick or on account of pain in his own household, but that, in the case of the prayer which is fixed for the whole congregation, even the individual may recite it in any language. And there are those who say that even the individual voicing his own needs may do so in any language he desires, except in Aramaic. (7)

Those and similar quotations from the literature of **halakhah** were first brought into the discussion by Eliezer Liebermann, in his two pamphlets defending the Berlin services of Israel Jacobson, published in 1818, **Or Nogah** ("Shining Light"). in which he states his own position, and **Nogah Hatzedeq** ("The Splendour of Righteousness"), a collection of rabbinic responsa in support of Jacobson's reforms, edited by him. It should be pointed out here that Liebermann's two pamphlets also adduced **halakhic** support for the introduction of the organ. (8)

Contrary to what has frequently been stated by some writers, Liebermann's works were meant as a halakhic defense of Jacobson's **Berlin** services, and **not** of those of the Hamburg Temple. **Or Nogah** and **Nogah Hatzedeq** were published in 1818. The Hamburg Temple prayerbook did not make its appearance until 1819. But when the Orthodox rabbinate of Hamburg reacted to Liebermann's defense of liturgical reforms in its 1819 responsa collection, **Eleh Divrei Haberit**, it not only tried to refute the halakhic arguments adduced by Liebermann and his respondents, but it also showed itself aware of the very near and present challenge presented by the Hamburg Temple and its recently published prayerbook. That fact might have led to the modern confusion of associating Liebermann's work with the Hamburg Temple.

On the basis of **Or Nogah** and **Nogah Hatzedeq**, as well as of **Eleh Divrei Haberit**, a literary warfare began, with both sides appealing to halakhic sources to support their respective positions. That warfare was renewed when the second edition of the Hamburg Temple prayerbook appeared in 1841, and periodically thereafter, whenever some major German Jewish community was in the process of considering the adoption of a reformed prayerbook. (9)

The historian Heinrich Graetz, certainly no friend of the rising Reform movement, writing about that literary warfare, was compelled by the evidence in hand to concede the victory in that literary warfare to the Reformers. He wrote:

> "The reasons which the (Orthodox) rabbis had adduced against the worship service of the (Hamburg) Temple were mostly not valid, and some of them were downright childish. The letter (of the Law) was against them (i.e., the Orthodox). The multiplicity of rabbinic authorities, belonging to such different times and countries, always enabled one to bring apparent proofs for and against a specific case. The rabbis should have said that, even though the letter could be adduced in favor of the innovations, the spirit of Talmudic Judaism must nevertheless condemn them. But they did not stand on that level; and, in their desire to utilize the letter, too, for their position, they revealed many a weakness." (10)

Something very similar had already been expressed by Zacharias Frankel, later to become famous as the founder of Conservative Judaism, when, in 1841, while he was Chief Rabbi of Dresden, he had been asked about his views on the second edition of the Hamburg Temple prayerbook and on the "Proclamation" issued by Hamburg's Orthodox rabbi, Haham Isaac Bernays, against the use of that prayerbook. Frankel made it abundantly clear that he personally did not like that prayerbook. He missed in it "the holiest sentiments of the nation" as well as a scientific principle, consistently applied. At the same time, he denied Bernays the right to condemn that prayerbook on **halakhic** grounds, and he insisted

(a) that all the prayers required by **tefilat hovah** (prayers deemed to be obligatory by the Talmud) are found in it, and (b) that "it has long been known and acknowledged" that the use of the German language for some of the prayers in the Hamburg Temple "does not constitute any injury to prayer." (11).

Both Gotthold Salomon, a preacher of the Temple and one of the editors of the second edition of the Hamburg Temple prayerbook, (12) and Samuel Holdheim, at that time Chief Rabbi of Mecklenburg-Schwerin, (13) attacked Frankel because of the subjectivity of his criticism. At the same time, they expressed their extreme satisfaction with Frankel's defense of the prayer book on **halakhic** grounds.

The knowledge that their liturgical reforms could be justified **halakhically** sustained not only the Hamburg Reformers, but also the editors of later Reform prayerbooks, who, in their departures from traditional liturgical formulae, had left the very moderate reforms of Hamburg far behind. Typical for that frame of mind is something which Isaac M. Wise did in his prayerbook, **Minhag America**. It has been customary for editors of traditional Jewish prayerbooks to preface their compendia with an abstract of the **halakhic** rules governing prayer, the **dinei tefillah**. (14) In his **Minhag America**, Wise did the same, -- although the particular **halakhic** selections he included were not necessarily those which an Orthodox editor of a prayerbook would choose. Preceding the text of the prayers in **Minhag America**, there is a page of **unvocalized** Hebrew, without either an English or a German translation, under the heading of: **dinim hashayakhim lehilkhot tefillah**, i.e., "Rules Applying to the Laws of Prayer". (15) Wise's "Rules" consist of the following quotations:

(1) **Shulhan Arukh, Orah Hayyim** 1:1 :

A man should be strong as a lion to arise in the morning to the service of his Creator.

(2) **Shulhan Arukh, Orah Hayyim** 1:4 :

Better is a little entreaty for divine grace, said with devotion (**kawwanah**), than much without devotion.

(3) **Abot** 3:18 :

Rabbi Simeon said: "Be careful with the recitation of the **Shema** and with the Prayer (of the Eighteen Benedictions); and when you pray, do not make your prayer a matter of fixed routine, but rather an appeal for mercy and grace before God, as it is said: For He is gracious and merciful, long-suffering and abundant in love, etc."

(4) **Abot** 4:4 :

Rabbi Eliezer said: "One who makes his prayer a matter of routine, his prayer is no appeal for divine grace."

(5) **Shulhan Arukh, Orah Hayim** 101:4 :

One can pray in whatever language one wants.

(6) **Shulhan Arukh, Orah Hayim** 62:2 :

One can recite the **Shema** in any language.

A few observations on Wise's "Rules Applying to the Laws of Prayer" may be permitted here.

(a) We are struck by the fact that those "Rules" are printed in unvocalized and untranslated Hebrew. While it is indeed possible that the laity, for whom **Minhag America** was intended, included **some** people who could read and understand unvocalized Hebrew, it is not very likely that the number of those people was very large. The suspicion, therefore, arises that the function of those "Rules" was rather to disarm any potential (and expected) Orthodox opposition to those departures from Tradition which Wise had permitted himself in his prayer book. Wise must have believed that those departures from the traditional ritual were justified by the principles inherent in his quotations from the **Talmud** and the **Shulhan Arukh**. They are, of course, passages which had been used by the European Reformers in their appeal to **halakhah** ever since **Or Nogah** and **Nogah Hatzedeq** in 1818.

(b) When Wise quoted the **halakhic** permission to pray in whatever language one wants, he and most nineteenth-century Reformers (with the exception of Samuel Holdheim and Mendel Hess) invoked a blanket dispensation of which they had no intention whatsoever to make full use. For the principle invoked would cover a worship service conducted altogether in the vernacular. Yet, with a few vernacular prayers, to be spoken here and there by the rabbi, even Geiger's two prayerbooks, of 1854 and 1870, were meant for a practically all-Hebrew worship service. So, for that matter, was Wise's own **Minhag America**. In fact, Wise, while encouraging **individual** prayer in the vernacular, insisted strongly that communal worship be conducted in the Hebrew language. He wrote in 1862: "Hymns, prayers, sermon in English, but the main portion of the divine service must remain in Hebrew **kedei shello tishtakah torah miyisrael** (so that the Torah not be forgotten in Israel)." (16)

(c) There is something somewhat paradoxical in the fondness which Wise and all other nineteenth-century Reformers had for the **halakhic** provision, going back to the Mishnah itself, that the **Shema** can be recited in any language. For if there was one part of the worship service which was recited in Hebrew even in the most radical Reform services, including those of Holdheim, it was the **Shema**! One would assume, therefore, that what was implied here was some kind of **qal vahomer**, the talmudic argument "from minor to major" or "from major to minor," as if to say: if even in the case of the **Shema**, which is one of the most important components of the Jewish worship service, we are permitted to use the vernacular, then how much the more would that permission apply to rubrics of a lesser degree of importance!

Again, it should be noted that there was no "Liberal **Halakhah**,", however we might care to define it, which was available at that time. Isaac M. Wise, like the European Reformers before him, appealed to the **halakhah**, -- on the basis of the sources which his Orthodox opponents, too, had to recognize as authoritative. Graetz was right, after all, when he said: "The multiplicity of rabbinic authorities, belonging to such different times and countries, always enabled one to bring apparent proofs for and against a specific case." (17) What could be said, perhaps, is that the Reformers and the Orthodox picked different components of the common **halakhic** tradition, -- the Reformers being the **meqilin**, the liberal, and the Orthodox being the **mahmirin**, the more stringent interpreters of the Law. To that extent, therefor, and to that extent only, one might be justified in speaking about a "Liberal **Halakhah**."

At the same time, it is obvious that neither side ever managed to convince the other. That may also be the reason why,in the twentieth century, there has not been much of a continuation of the literary battle between the Reformers and the Orthodox in the arena of liturgical reform. As we have shown elsewhere, the old battle of the **halakhic** proof-texts was succeeded for a while by new battle lines drawn up in the field of **Wissenschaft des Judentums**, the scientific and historical study and Judaism, -- to the extent to which that discipline could be invoked by way of either justifying or attacking liturgical reforms. (18)

Moreover, the invocation of **halakhic** sources, and, as a consequence, the full development of what might be called a "Liberal **Halakhah**" had become highly problematical, once the traditional belief in the divine revelation of Scripture, still shared by men like Wise and Holdheim, not to mention the belief in God's role in the shaping of the rabbinic tradition, had been jettisoned by succeeding generations of Reform rabbis. Indeed, it often looks as though the work of the German Rabbinical Conferences of 1844, 1845 and 1846, in laying the foundations for a liberalization of the **halakhah**, without, at the same time, denying the **halakhah's** validity in principle, has been carried on, in America, by the Conservative movement, rather than by Reform Judaism.

Conceivably, one might reach a consensus about liturgical practice, and Reform or Liberal congregations of a given country might even issue a unified liturgy, as happened in the United States with the **Union Prayer Book** in 1894, and in Germany with the **Einheitsgebetbuch** in 1929. But such unified liturgies do not necessarily imply a sense of responsibility towards the **halakhic** heritage of the Jewish past.

The **Einheitsgebetbuch** clearly showed such a sense of responsibility; the **Union Prayer Book did** so only in a rather attenuated form. In any case, liturgical consensus, with or without a sense of responsibility towards the **halakhic** heritage of the Jewish past, is not yet, in and by itself, **halakhah**. **Halakhah**, is more than a catalogue of common practices; it also requires the belief that, in some sense, which need not be a Fundamentalist one, those practices are related to an affirmed divine Revelation. (19) And a movement which issues a prayerbook, on a number of pages of which any reference to God has been studiously avoided -- in order to placate the agnostic or atheistic susceptibilities of some of its laity and even some of its clergy --, would hardly seem to provide the kind of setting in which serious talk about **halakhah**, rather than folkways or customs, is in order.

All of which is not to say that one could not have a fairly traditional liturgy even **without** an affirmation of **halakhah**. Perhaps in one sense the most "traditional" Reform liturgy ever produced was that of the West London Synagogue of British Jews in the 1840's. It included a volume devoted, **inter alia**, to the Ninth of Ab, the Fast of Gedaliah, the Tenth Day of Tebet, the Seventeenth Day of Tammuz, and the Redemption of the First Born. (20)

Such a volume, I feel confident in stating after examing hundreds of Reform and Liberal liturgies, must be absolutely unique among the liturgical productions of Liberal and Reform Judaism. Yet the West London Synagogue of British Jews, at the time when it created its original liturgy, had no use for rabbinic **halakhah** at all. (21) Its antipathy towards rabbinic Judaism was so strong that it could not get itself to recite the **qaddish** in Aramaic, the **lingua franca** of Rabbinic Judaism. A Hebrew version of that prayer was produced instead. And, while that congregation accepted the biblical commandment about the "four species" on the Feast of Tabernacles, it could not get itself to call the festival bouquet by its Rabbinic name, **lulav**, preferring to reword the traditional benediction **'al netilath lulav** as follows: "Blessed art thou, O Lord our God, King of the Universe, who hast sanctified us with thy commandments, and commanded us to take the fruit of goodly trees, branches of palm-trees, boughs of thick trees, and willows of the brook." (22) That benediction, by the way, was recited in Hebrew.

Yet with all of its rejection of rabbinic formulations and nomenclature, which, I suspect, must have included the very name of **halakhah**, that British Reform congregation prayed for the coming of a personal Messiah, the Ingathering of the Exiles in Zion, the Rebuilding of the Jerusalem Temple, and even the Restoration of the Sacrificial Cult! One could, in other words, adhere to Tradition, both in theology and in liturgy, without, at the same time, subjecting oneself to rabbinically mediated **halakhah**.

But nineteenth-century British Reform Judaism was **sui generis** in this respect; and it has thoroughly revised its quasi-Karaite stance in the twentieth century. Other branches of Reform Judaism, far less violent in their rejection of Rabbinism than the West London Synagogue was, have nevertheless managed to depart to a far greater extent than nineteenth-century British Reform did from both traditional beliefs and their expression in the liturgical forms of the past.

Would it, then, be true to say that, whatever might have been the case in the nineteenth century, the framers and users of Liberal liturgy have by now outgrown the need for a Liberal **halakhah**? My own inclination is to answer that question in the negative, and that for two reasons:

First of all, it may well be that, while there is no static corpus which has been handed down to us from the past with a label reading "Liberal **Halakhah**" attached to it, there could, in fact, well be an evolving consensus among Liberal Jews about the format and the contents of Jewish worship. That, indeed, for a rather long time, had been one of the felicitous by-products of the old **Union Prayer Book**, which breathed a common commitment to the God of Israel, Ethical Monotheism, and the Mission of Israel, while allowing for variety in the expression of a number of different themes in different services. That consensus has been shattered by the last American Reform prayerbook, which attempts to cater to believers and non-believers alike. But perhaps, one day, American Reform Jews may unite again in common religious affirmations, and their liturgy might then again reflect a Liberal Jewish consensus about the format and the contents of Jewish worship.

Another starting-point for a "Liberal **Halakhah**" in matters liturgical might be the collecting of **minhagim** (local liturgical practices) in use among Reform Jews, just as our own beloved Dr. Freehof, in whose honor we have gathered, has rendered yeoman service in bringing together the practices of Reform Jews, and in determining their relation to the halakhic sources of old. Of course, a collection of **minhagim is not** yet a compendium of **halakhah**. But it could, one day, become **halakhah** once two things happen: if those **minhagim** really and truly become generally accepted practice, and if a theological basis is found to link those practices with the thought that those who carry out those practices are, in some way or another, fulfilling a **mitzvah**, that is to say, implementing God's will for Jews in the "here and now."

I am not saying that our liturgical **minhagim** all deserve to become common practice, or that our theology has already advanced sufficiently to provide the creedal basis which alone would make the concept of **halakhah** meaningful. I am, in fact, advocating a rather careful screening of those **minhagim**, lest we sanctify something which should be described as **minhag sh'tut**, a custom without rhyme or reason.

In that particular category, for example, I would place the custom now rapidly spreading in many Reform and also some Conservative synagogues, of opening the Ark each time the "Adoration" is recited. Opening the Ark for the **alenu** prayer within the **musaph** benedictions of the High Holy Days represented one of the most dramatic moments of the traditional High Holy Day services. Lifting that custom out of its High Holy Day setting and turning it into a weekly or even daily routine, not only weakens the dramatic effect of a unique High Holy Day observance, but, on account of its constant re-enactment, it also ultimately fails to inspire during Sabbath and weekday services.

Similarly, we are witnessing the creation of all kinds of novel observances, which invariably imitate the format of the Passover **seder**. This not only robs the **seder** of its dramatic effect on Passover, but it also creates the impression that we Jews are so poor in religious imagination and creativity that the only form of celebration we can ever think of is that in which the Passover is celebrated.

All of which is to say that some of our **minhagim** are in urgent need of scrutiny before we can consider them as the basis of a Liberal **halakhah** in the area of liturgy. That is why, at this particular moment, such a Liberal **halakhah** is as yet but a future expectation, -- hoped for by some, dreaded by others.

The scrutiny of **minhagim**, to which I have

alluded as a desideratum, brings me to the second reason why I think that the framers and users of Liberal liturgy have not outgrown the need for a Liberal **halakhah**, and that such a Liberal **halakhah** is indeed something towards which we ought to be striving.

It should be understood that not all areas of **halakhah** need to have the same structure or breathe the same spirit. We would all agree, for example, that the **halakhah** dealing with murder and robbery is a different sort of **halakhah** from the one that is concerned with the details of erecting a proper **sukkah** on the Feast of Tabernacles, or that the **hilkhot Shabbat**, the laws governing proper Sabbath observance, are different in tone from the **halakhah** which regulates the Purim dinner. There are regulations, and there are regulations. There is law, and there is law. How, then, would we characterize the **halakhah** of Liturgy?

Some of the nineteenth-century German Protestant scholars who became experts in Judaic Studies, the Webers and Boussets, the Schuerers and Billerbecks, could not criticize rabbinic Judaism enough, -- because rabbinic Judaism had made such an intimate act as praying to our Father who is in Heaven a matter of legalistic debate and codification of rules. How far can one go, they protested, in stultifying the spontaneous outpourings of the pious human heart! (23) (One suspects that Catholic scholars may have been a little more charitable, seeing that they have their own rather considerable liturgical **halakhah**.) But what those nineteenth-century Protestant scholars (and some Reform Jews who were influenced by them) failed to see is that much of rabbinic **halakhah** dealing with liturgy is not so much a matter of statutory legislation as it is a compendium of liturgical **aesthetics**. When there is an argument in **B**. Berakhot llb, for example, as to whether Scriptural verses quoted in prayer can or cannot be changed by employing a euphemism in place of a Scriptural expression felt to be rather crass for liturgical use, only a Philistine would think of it in terms of a heartless legalism, rather than an attempt to establish the aesthetics of worship. When the **halakhah** of liturgy states that two juxtaposed prayers cannot both begin with the words, "Blessed art Thou, O Lord," the **halakhah is** incorporating an aesthetic preference, rather than an item of cold legislation. (24) And when the **halakhah** insists that certain inserts for Hanukkah and New Moon be inserted in a given prayer before the concluding eulogy (**hatimah**) of that prayer is recited, (25) then that provision is due to no arbitrary rabbinic wiles, but to the rabbinic refusal, based on a sense of liturgical aesthetics, to have prayers, as it were, artlessly floating around in the liturgy without an appropriate conclusion. Prayerbooks like **Gates of Prayer** which ignore that provision, (26) may be intended to express their editors' independence from past rabbinic dicta; but they also call into question those editors' aesthetic sense. Nor was it anything other than a sense for the fitness of things when the ancient rabbis ruled that, on Purim, the reading of the Scroll of Esther takes the place of the singing of the Hallel Psalms, clearly indicating that the Purim mood differs from the aura of solemnity normally associated with Psalms 113 - 118, -- this, too, being a rabbinic ruling ignored in Gates of Prayer. (27)

We could go on and on, listing examples of how the traditional **halakhah** of liturgy addresed itself time and again to issues of aesthetics. But what has already been mentioned should suffice. If, then, liturgical **halakhah** in the past concerned itself with the aesthetics of worship, it is clear that we Reform Jews today would fare much better than we have done in the recent past, if we had a modern Liberal **halakhah** of liturgy to guide us in our future liturgical efforts, -- if, that is to say, we could agree on certain criteria of good taste in producing the next edition of our prayerbook.

In making this statement, I am aware of the fact that it is notoriously difficult to win universal approval for criteria of good taste and standards of aesthetics. Yet that is precisely what the ancient rabbis managed to do for the aesthetics of Jewish worship. They did it for their time, and it proved to be helpful to many later generations. We today may have to do some reformulating, but we should set about doing so with the same sense of reverence and awe of the "beauty of holiness" which has guided earlier shapers of liturgical **halakhah**. But it is precisely along those lines that, one day, it might really make sense to speak about "Liberal **Halakhah** and Liturgy."

Notes

1. Meyer Israel Bresselau, one of the editors of the 1819 edition of the Hamburg Temple prayerbook, said: "We wanted to improve the worship service, and that has happened. I do not feel called upon to be a reformer." Cf. Caesar Seligmann, Zur Entstehungsgeschichte des Hamburger Tempels," in **Liberales Judentum**, September/October 1918, p. 72. Gotthold Salomon, one of the editors of the second (1841) edition of the Hamburg Temple prayerbook, wrote a pamphlet against Haham Isaac Bernays, the Orthodox Hamburg rabbi who had issued a Proclamation" against the use of that prayerbook. Gotthold Salomon, **Das neue Gebetbuch und seine Verketzerung**. Hamburg, 1841. The burden of

Salomon's pamphlet is the demonstration that, contrary to the accusations levelled by Bernays, the traditional doctrines of redemption, of the coming of a personal Messiah, and of the Resurrection of the Dead can indeed all be found in the new prayerbook.

2. Quoted by Eliezer Liebermann, in **Or Nogah,** Dessau, 1818, p.2.

3. Quoted by Liebermann in **Or Nogah**, p. 5, and by Aaron Chorin in Eliezer Liebermann, ed., **Nogah Hatzedeq**. Dessau, 1818, p. 17.

4. This is a precis of the responsum found in Blau's edition, Vol. II, pp. 469 - 476. It was known to the early Reformers in the form of a quotation by David ben Zimra, in his Responsum #94. Quoted by Liebermann **Or Nogah**, p. 13.

5. Quoted by Liebermann **Or Nogah**, p. 4.

6. Quoted by Liebermann in **Or Nogah**, p. 4, and by Chorin in Liebermann's **Nogah Hatzedeq**, p. 16.

7. Quoted by Liebermann in **Or Nogah**, p. 4, and by Chorin in Liebermann's **Nogah Hatzedeq**, p. 17.

8. For the arguments, see Jakob J. Petuchowski, art. "Organ -- in the 19th and 20th Centuries," in **Encyclopaedia Judaica**, Vol. 12, cols. 1454 - 1455.

9. Cf. Jakob J. Petuchowski, **Prayerbook Reform in Europe**. New York World Union for Progressive Judaism, 1968, pp. 31 - 43, 49 - 58, 84 - 104.

10. Heinrich Graetz, **Geschichte der Juden**, Vol. XI. Second Edition, revised by M. Brann, Leipzig, 1900, pp. 396f.

11. Zacharias Frankel, "Schreiben an die Direction des Tempelvereins," in **Der Orient**, V. III (1842), pp. 53ff., 61ff., 71ff.

12. Gotthold Salomon, **Sendschreiben an den Herrn Dr. Z. Frankel**, 1842.

13. Samuel Holdheim, **Verketzerung und Gewissensfreiheit. Ein Zweites Votum in dem Hamburger Tempelstreit.** Schwerin, 1842, pp. 89-111.

14. Cf., e.g., Seligman Isaac Baer, ed., **Seder**

Avodat Yisrael. Roedelheim, 1868, pp. 10 - 15.

15. Isaac M. Wise, ed., **Minhag America** (1873 edition), V. I, p. 3. This page was already contained in the first edition of 1852.

16. Isaac M. Wise in **The Israelite**, V. IX, November 14, 1862, p. 148.

17. See above, Note #10.

18. Cf. Petuchowski, **Prayerbook Reform in Europe**. pp. 100 - 103.

19. Cf. Jakob J. Petuchowski, "Problems of Reform Halacha," in Bernard Martin, ed., **Contemporary Reform Jewish Thought**. Chicago, Quadrangle Books, 1968, pp. 105 - 122.

20. David W. Marks and Albert Lowy, ed., **Forms of Prayer used in the West London Synagogue of British Jews**, Vol. V ("Prayers for various Occasions"). London, J. Wertheimer & Co., 5603 (=1842).

21. Cf. Jakob J. Petuchowski, "Karaite Tendencies in an Early Reform Haggadah," in **H.U.C.A.**, V. XXI (1960), pp. 223 - 249.

22. **Forms of Prayer used in the West London Synagogue of British Jews**. V. II ("Prayers for the Festivals"). Fourth Edition. London, Williams, Lea & Co., 1921, p. 42.

23. Cf., e.g., Ferdinand Weber, **System der altsynagogalen palaestinischen Theologie**. Leipzig, 1880, pp. 41f.

24. See **B**. Berakhot 46a.

25. See **B**. Shabbat 24a.

26. Cf. Gates of Prayer, pp. 137 and 138ff.

27. See **B**. Megillah 14a, and cf. Gates of Prayer p. 71, for the instruction to recite a short version of Hallel on Purim.

Chapter II

Reform Responsa: Developing a Theory of Liberal **Halakhah**

Peter J. Haas

The phrase "Reform **halakhah**" seems to be an oxymoron. **halakhah**, after all, is the corpus of norms that make up traditional rabbinic Judaism, the single correct way in which social and religious problems are to be defined, analyzed and adjudicated by the holy people of Israel. In fact, since the late eighteenth century, the word **halakhah** has come to be somewhat synonymous with Orthodox praxis. This is precisely, however, what Reform Judaism was originally formed to protest. If there is any hallmark of the Reform tradition, it is the rejection not only of particular Orthodox **halakhot** -- norms -- but of the whole concept that there can be, are, or ought to be such a system of absolute norms in the first place. How then are we to make any sense of a phrase like "Reform **halakhah**"?

In what follows I hope to throw some light on what the oxymoron "Reform **halakhah**" has meant in our movement. I propose to do so not from a philosophical perspective: what meaning can these words have when used in juxtaposition, but from an historical one. That is, I propose to find out what "Reform **halakhah**" is by examining the phenomenon of Reform **halakhic** processes over the last century and a half. I do not intend to pass judgment whether the process is good, bad, efficient or even self-contradictory. I mean to examine the date and see what has in fact been going on. This will allow us at least to characterize what the Reform **halakhic** process has been up to now. Only with this data before us can we venture to pass evaluative judgments on it.

Before proceeding, let me define what I mean by Reform **halakhic** processes. What I am referring to is the activity on the part of Reform rabbis of writing responsa from the perspective of Reform Judaism and with the purpose of guiding Reform Jews. Responsa are, of course, the quintessential literature of **halakhah**. In a responsum, the rabbinic authority attempts to fashion a definitive answer to some question of Judaic behavior by collating and analyzing past normative writings. The published result of this exercise is meant to tell the recipient what he or she ought to do. That is, the implicit assumption of a responsum is that the answer it adduces will be taken by the addressee as an authoritative statement of what Judaism requires in this particular case. Or, to put matters differently, the addresses is expected to act according to the proclamation of the responsum because a) the responsum represents the opinion of an authority the addressee has recognized and b) this authority has demonstrated that the rendered opinion is in fact continuous with Judaic tradition. Since Reform, by definition, rejects the notion of a single monolithic system of **halakhah** extending from Sinai and since it rejects the normativity of basic **halakhic** sources such as the **Shulhan Arukh**, and since Reform does not recognize the authority of the rabbinate to include the right to issue normative rulings that bind the individual congregant, the continuation of the responsa-writing tradition in Reform Judaism is unexpected and surprising. It is the existence of this genre in Reform that draws me to the phrase "Reform **halakhah**" at all. To understand what that phrase might mean, then, we must begin, it seems to me, with the literature that reflects the very heart of **halakhah** - the responsa that have been routinely produced by the Reform movement.

Two characteristics of the Reform responsa tradition should be noted at the outset. The first is that responsa have been part of the Reform movement from the very beginning. Jacob Petuchowski, for example, has shown that the very earliest manifestations of the reforming movement in German Judaism at the turn of the last century revolved around changes in the prayerbook, and that many of these changes were explained, challenged and defended through responsa. (1) The second is that the character of these responsa within the Reform movement has not remained stable, but has changed considerably over the last 150 to 200 years (as it has in Orthodoxy, too, by the way). In studying Reform responsa, then, we must not look at all texts as the same. Rather, we much recognize that considerable changes have occurred in the style and character of Reform responsa-writing over time, each style representing a particular nuance in the writer's understanding of the **halakhic** process as this relates to Reform Judaism. We thus have before us not a tradition of Reform responsa-writing, but a number of eras of Reform responsa-writing, each with its own conception of what I am calling "Reform **halakhah**." It is to these various conceptions that I now want to draw your attention.

In what follows, I shall divide the literary history of Reform responsa-writing into three epochs. The first might in fact be called the pre-history of Reform responsa-writing. I am thinking here of a collection of diverse Reform responsa gathered together and published under the name **Noga Hatzedeq** in Dessau in 1818. The writers represented in this volume, which includes **Derekh Haqodesh** by Joseph Hayyim ben Sasson, **Ya'ir Nativ** by Jacob Recanati, **Kin'at Haemet** by Aaron Chorin and a long essay entitled **Or Noga** by Eliezer Lieberman, were all sympathetic to the reforming experiments going on that time in Berlin and Hamburg. The writings collected here deal with many of the reforms being instituted: reading the **Torah** rather than chanting it, the use of organ music, the inclusion of prayers in the vernacular and the like. I categorize this responsa collection as part of Reform responsa-writing because its content is clearly and self-consciously devoted to adducing **halakhic** precedent for the liturgical reforms of the Berlin and Hamburg congregations. That is, all of the arguments set forth in these documents reflect basic Reform sensibilities. I nonetheless want to argue that this curious volume is part of the "pre-history" of Reform responsa and not an example of Reform responsa-writing proper. I say this because the mode of argument and rhetoric here remains well within the traditional style of responsa-writing. That is, there is nothing "reform" about the **way** the arguments are framed in these essays, although the arguments themselves are clearly reform-minded. The authors represented in **Noga Hatzedeq** have, we might say, poured Reform content into older literary wineskins. Unfortunately, by doing so they sealed their own fate. The content of these responsa was, of course, rejected by traditionalists and the form, as we shall see, was rejected by the Reform movement. Before I develop this thought, however, let me finish my summation of what I conceive to be the history of Reform responsa-writing.

The second and third epochs of Reform

responsa-writing see the evolution of a new form of responsa composition that takes account of the radically new meaning and purpose of what they contain. One group of such responsa was published in Germany during the early 1840's. They make up our second epoch. Included here are two collections that appear, significantly for our purposes, in the vernacular - **Theologische Gutachten ueber das Gebetbuch nach dem Gebrauch des Neuen Israelitischen Tempelverein in Hamburg** (2) and **Rabbinische Gutachten ueber die Vertraeglichkeit der freien Forschung mit dem Rabbineramte.** (3) With the publication of the latter, German Reform responsa cease to be written, and our second epoch has played itself out.

The third epoch takes place in America. It begins with the position papers that were published in the Yearbook of the CCAR under the imprimatur of the so-called "Responsa Committee." The first of these appeared, if I am not mistaken, in 1913 (4) and continue to be written in our own day. They have achieved by now more than a mere in-house readership with the prolific publications of Dr. Freehof who chaired the CCAR Responsa Committee from 1954 to 1976 and with a collection of pre-Freehofian American Reform responsa by Walter Jacob in **American Reform Responsa.** (5) While the second epoch, that of the German Reform responsa, enjoyed but a short lifespan, the American Reform responsa tradition is approaching its centenary (the Responsa Committee was appointed in 1906) (6) and appears to be still gaining in energy. This suggests that traditional modes of **halakhic** discourse - responsa - on the one hand, and Reform Judaism (at least in its American style) on the other are not incompatible. Yet the successful Reform responsa of America do represent a particular style or form of responsa-writing. We shall return to the question of what this is in a few minutes. Before I can evaluate the American Reform responsa style, however, I need to place it into its historical context.

Let me turn back, then to the material I mentioned earlier, namely the first two epochs of Reform responsa. I said just a few minutes ago that the earliest Reform responsa, represented by the collection **Noga Hatzedeq**, were really no different than normal Orthodox responsa of their time in rhetoric or discursive style. While their content was quite different, their mode of presenting that content was hardly new. I also suggested that that was why they ultimately failed. To clarify what I mean, I will need to review what exactly the traditional responsa genre was and how **Noga Hatzedeq** fit in.

In some sense it is an oversimplification to talk about a single responsa genre at all. Responsa emerge in rabbinic literature some time after the completion of the **Babylonian Talmud** in the seventh century. When precisely they began is a matter of some debate; in fact some scholars claim they date back to King David. (7) The fact is that actual responsa only survive from about the eighth century, and they are so rudimentary, often only a question followed by a one or two word decision, that it is hard to imagine that they represent a long previous literary tradition. It seems much more likely to assume what the evidence in fact suggest, that responsa began in the post-Talmudic era. (8) Their purpose, it seems clear, was to provide outlying Jewish communities with a way of receiving authoritative interpretations or application decisions on Talmudic law from the very centers of Talmudic studies, the Gaonic academies in Babylonia. In essence, local leaders of farflung Jewish communities around the

Mediterranean basin would send written queries to the Babylonian Talmudic academies. These queries would be researched and answered, with a copy of the answer sent by post or courier back to the originating community. (9) In this way the literary genre of responsa seems to have begun.

The next stage in development occurred as the academies went into decline starting in the tenth century or so. At this same time, we witness the corresponding emergence of local rabbinic centers of learning in North Africa and southern Europe. Gradually, queries were directed more and more to local rabbis rather than to the distant Gaonic authorities in Babylonia. These local rabbis, in turn, began to author their responsa. By the Middle Ages, such responsa had become a major literary enterprise of local European and North African rabbis. (10) They dealt, of course, with every conceivable question and life situation. By the twelfth century a new dynamic began to take hold. As the number of rabbis grew and as rabbinic learning matured and deepened, responsa became not only a tool for the development of **halakhah**, but actually a forum for the display of individual rabbi's intellectual virtuosity. That is, responsa became more and more excuses for intellectual gymnastics, occasions for citing Scripture and **Talmud** and then interpreting them in innovative and highly complex ways. By the late Orthodox period, that is from the late seventeenth and early eighteenth century on, this process reached a sort of logical conclusion: the argument itself - the display of rabbinic virtuosity - had become an end in itself. There was still a question to be answered, and an answer usually did emerge, but the bulk of the text, by now often some 20 pages or more, was devoted to argumentation itself, an intricate Arabesque of citations from all rabbinic literature,

Scripture, **Talmud**, **midrash**, other responsa, etc, detailed and even hairsplitting analyses (**pilpul**) and general overviews of an entire area of legal and moral speculation, all conducted in the complex artificial academic language of Talmudo-rabbinic Hebrew. (11) The practical answer was often buried in the author's overwhelming display of erudition and on occasion even appeared as a sort of afterthought. This was the nature of the responsa genre as it had developed at the time the Reform movement began to take shape.

The responsa collected in **Noga Hatzedeq** fall within this general late pattern. They are prolix and flowery, they cite numerous rabbinic sources even when these are redundant or not quite to the point, and they wander off into rhetorical gymnastics. Aaron Choriner in his comprehensive responsum on liturgical reforms, **Kin' at Haemet** even resorts to erudite wordplays to sustain his argument. (12) Each, of course, addresses itself to certain **halakhic** questions. **Kin' at Haemet**, for example, proposes to deal with three questions in particular: whether or not later additions to the prayerbook may be removed, whether or not an organ can be used to accompany worship and whether or not prayers may be said in the vernacular. A fourth question proposes to explore the possibility of change at all. So, as I said, what Aaron Choriner and others were doing is what we might precisely expect; using the standard rabbinic literary vehicle, the responsa, to argue in rabbinic style their own views on how Judaism ought to be done.

The irony, of course, is that the precise values that sustained this Orthodox literary genre were those that were under attack by Reform with the aid of people like Aaron Choriner. The lay reformers in Hamburg and Berlin were not interested in being led by prodigies in Talmudic learning or in intricate applications of rules mined from the vast legal codes of Medieval Jewry. They saw themselves in a new world in which modern secular cultures was vastly superior to anything people had known before. It was also a world in which spiritual truths were more important to their religious self-identify than traditional legalisms and in which modern science - **Wissenschaft** - was deemed more reliable than medieval **pilpul** in arriving at truth. In short, the virtues stressed by the new reformers were not the virtues of the classical responsa literature. It should come as no surprise, then, that the type of responsa authored by Chorin and others failed to resonate among later reformers. Their mode of discourse reflected an entirely different universe of values. The medieval form of their responsa clashed with their modernist content.

This brings me to the next epoch, the first responsa written well within the Reform movement for the Reform movement, and in a style that took shape in the context of the German Reform movement. I am referring now to the two German language publications mentioned earlier: **Theologische Gutachten das Gebetbuch nach dem Gebrauch des Neuen Israelitischen Tempelverein in Hamburg** and **Rabbinische Gutachten ueber die Vertraeglichkeit der freien Forschung mit dem Rabbineramte**.

Let me turn first to the **Theologische Gutachten**. The book, as its title makes clear, claims to be a collection of responsa (**Gutachten**). Yet this collection is unusual, and so indicative of the self-understanding of the early German Reform movement, in a number of ways. First of all, the writings are in German, not in the rabbinic Hebrew that characterized, and still characterized, traditional responsa. This detail of language is significant. Responsa traditionally, I would argue, are seen as sacred writings issued by holy men. They are extensions of the **Talmud** which is itself connected to **halakhah lemosheh misinai** - the law given to Moses at Sinai. Responsa then by nature had to be written in the technical and holy language of the rabbinic estate. To write responsa in German therefore represents a rather substantial revision in perception. As responsa, the writings in this volume mean to identify themselves with rabbinic literature, but as "**Gutachten**" they are part of a new universe of secular literature. Classical rabbinic literature belongs to an intellectual culture which, because of its language, claims to transcend time and place. The **Gutachten**, on the other hand, identify themselves explicitly with a particular mundane society.

Second, the collection is not made up of a series of responses composed by a single rabbi to a number of questions submitted to him -- the pattern we find in the classical responsa-literature. Rather, the book is a series of essays written by a number of rabbis (12 in all) that speak to a single general issue. The issue in this case is a general ban issued by Hacham Isaac Bernays, leader of the Ashkenazic community in Hamburg, against the new edition of the Hamburg Temple's (Reform) prayerbook. (13) The **Gutachten** presented to the reader are not designed to adduce Jewish law so much as to argue an ideological or theological point in response to Bernay's proclamation.

This brings me to a third point. One of the definitive characteristics of responsa since at least the tenth century has been their citation of rabbinic sources. In fact by the High Middle Ages, as I said, response are often little more than strings of citations from rabbinic literature joined together by patches of argumentation. This pattern is not at all evident in any of the diverse **Gutachten** in this volume. Citations of rabbinic literature, say **Talmud**, are few and far between. The weight of the argument is carried by invoking general philosophical and theological principles about what worship is or ought to be, about religious feelings and sensibilities and about the central truth of Judaism that stands above the historically shaped nature of Jewish communities. References to **Talmud, Shulkhan Arukh** and other rabbinic writings do exist in these **Gutachten**, but they are, as I said, few, far between, and not central to the discourse.

To sum it up, then, we find that on a purely formal level this collection of **Gutachten** moves away from the classical pattern of responsa writings in significant ways. These are not in the classical rabbinic language but in German, a secular language. Secondly, they do not cite or develop rabbinic law, but focus instead on the philosophical question of the nature of modern religious sensibility. And, third, they are examples of philosophical discourse, not a web constructed out of citations of the holy literature.

This, of course, represents a completely new understanding of how the interior conversation of Judaism is to take shape. Development within Judaism is no longer the bailiwick of the parochially schooled rabbis who read and write in their own holy language and who draw on only their own tradition to address new needs. The **Gutachten** reveal an entirely new conviction, namely that Judaic discourse must take place within the larger linguistic and cultural universe of the modern world. The authorities draw not so much on traditional wisdom as on modern philosophy and theology. Jewish tradition makes its presence felt, but in a clearly secondary way. We witness here, it seems, a ritual in which a general philosophical or theological argument is made "Jewish" by citing Judaic material at strategic points. **Talmud** is quoted not as a source of knowledge or truth but as a source of identity. I say this, at least in part, because citations from classical rabbinic texts are never central to the argument, and are at times even inappropriately cited. Let me give one or two examples.

In the final essay of the book, Leopold Stein argues that Bernays' proclamation was simply out of line. As proof he invokes the rabbinic maxim " **ein onshin ele mazhirin**" (One ought not punish but warn). (14) The statement as stated occurs nowhere in **Talmud**. Very similar statements do appear, however, in **B**. Zevahim 106b, for example. There the text is arguing that God in the **Torah** never establishes the punishment of utter extinction (**karet**) without first giving a written warning in **Torah**. This rather general view of how **Torah** relates to divine punishment is hardly comparable to the situation for which Stein uses the quote, namely to say that Bernays had no right to issue a **ban** against the prayerbook because he had not first issued a specific **warning** against using the second edition. The citation gives an aura of Talmudic sanction for Stein's point while being somewhat beside the point. A more blatant misuse of rabbinic authorities is committed by Joseph Aub. (15) Aub concedes that Bernays is technically correct in saying that one who does not say the prayer **Emet Veyatziv** (left out in the revised prayerbook) in the morning has not fulfilled his religious obligation. This comes straight from **B**. Berakhot 12a. Aub goes on to argue, however, that the tradition in fact has a more moderate side as well, and that the bald statement in Berakhot just cited is in essence rejected in the **Shulkhan Arukh**, O.H. 66: 10. On a superficial level Aub is correct. The **Shulkhan Arukh** says that one who omits this payer has not fulfilled his obligation, that is, properly. Isserles, who glosses the text and reports on the European conventions, goes on to explain that this applied only to one who was **forced** to omit this prayer, not one who skips it out of convenience. **Shulkhan Arukh**, then hardly supplies a warrant for omitting the prayer from the prayer book entirely, as Aub would have us believe. One final example occurs in the piece by Abraham Kohn. (16) Here he addresses Bernays' complaint that the new prayerbook is not kosher because it deletes all reference to an individual Messiah. Kohn now argues that in fact there is good solid precedence for this in the **Talmud**. He cites no less a figure than Hillel, who in **B**. Sanhedrin 99a says, "There is no Messiah for Israel!" The quote is accurate. Kohn goes on to suggest, however, that this view of Hillel prevails. This is simply not the case. Hillel's denial occurs in the middle of a conversation which continues to discuss the coming of the Messiah as if Hillel had never spoken; the other authorities of **Talmud** simply ignore the view given to Hillel. They, as well as later rabbinic tradition, apparently think the hope of an individual Messiah is not vain. Hillel's view here hardly reflects the rabbinic view, as Kohn would have us believe. Once again the attempt to use rabbinic literature to bolster the Reform arguments proves to be off-center. Yet I think this hardly matters in the long run. The citations are not substantive, but rhetorical; they are meant to give the text an aura of Jewishness.

Let me now quickly turn to the second responsa collection from this period, entitled **Rabbinische Gutachten ueber die Vertraeglichkeit**

der freien Forschung mit dem Rabbineramte. We may translate the title roughly as "rabbinic responsa concerning the compatibility of free research with the rabbinic office." The title is suggestive in two ways. First of all these are to be rabbinic responsa as opposed to the earlier theological responsa. We would expect then to find texts that more closely resemble classical responsa than did the academic essays in the previous volume. On the other hand, the rest of the title puts us on notice that the subject of the responsa will not be **halakhic** questions but a broader intellectual agendum. The title thus vacillates between responsa and academic essays. So, as it turns out, does the content.

The collection **Rabbinische Gutachten** appeared in 1842 and so is contemporary with the **Theologische Gutachten**. It was published as a response to an attack on one of the leaders of early Reform, Abraham Geiger. Abraham Geiger was appointed to the post of rabbi in Breslau in 1839. He was appointed specifically to serve the interests of the more reform-minded members of the community who found the senior rabbi of the community, Solomon Tiktin, to be unacceptable traditional and totally unsympathetic to their views. Tiktin not only resented Geiger's appointment as his associate, but was deeply antagonistic to the changes to which Geiger was committed. The clash of these two rabbis in Breslau became the focus of the religious struggle between Orthodoxy and Reform throughout Germany. Tiktin brought the dispute to full blows in 1841 with the publication of his **Darstellung** (17) in which he gathered together attacks on Reform in general and Geiger in particular from a number of traditionalist rabbis. In response, the Breslau community leaders solicited responses from rabbis sympathetic to Geiger and the program of reform.

Ten of these, with an introduction, became the **Rabbinische Gutachten**. A year later a second volume was published containing seven more such **Gutachten**. These, then, were documents written by liberal rabbis in response to the published Orthodox attacks on Geiger.

With this background in mind, we turn to the materials themselves. The argument here seems clearly to be between rabbis, with the general public allowed to listen in. I say this because, on the one hand, the authors feel compelled to cite rabbinic documents to a much greater degree than was the case in the **Theologische Gutachten**. In most cases, furthermore, the citations are in Hebrew, and at least two of the seventeen essays contain end notes that are entirely in Hebrew (those of Aaron Chorin and of Moses Gutmann). This seems to indicate that for at least some of the contributors, the primary audience was thought to be their fellow rabbis. On the other hand, these authors invariably translated the Hebrew passages into German, presumable so that the general reader could follow the argument. The invocation of classical rabbinic texts, especially **Talmud**, Maimonides, and **Shulkhan Arukh**, makes these essays much more "responsa-like" than those of **Theologische Gutachten**. Nor is this all. A number of contributors have cast their essays in a recognizably responsa-like form, with opening **sheelot** (questions) and pietistic conclusions. (18) So we can still see here a lingering attempt to appropriate the responsa-form for the needs of Reform. It is certainly suggestive that not only was this struggle to appropriate the responsa-form no longer evident in the second volume of **Rabbinische Gutachten**, but was never tried again within German reform. This was due, I assume, to the same forces that doomed **Noga Hatzedeq**. There was, I submit, a basic incompatibility between the German reform rabbinate and the attitudes or assumptions presupposed by the responsa form.

Let me now try briefly to spell out what I think this incompatibility is. Classical responsa are possible only if; you grant the authors certain assumptions. Basically responsa have to presuppose that the past proclamations of rabbinic culture are in some sense true or at least normative. Why else cite them as authorities? It also presupposes that the most important academic framework out of which the rabbi can speak, **as rabbi**, is the world of rabbinic learning. Finally, responsa assume that there is an answer to an individual's religious questions that can be found outside of that individual. The answer is to be found in the collective wisdom of the Jewish people that was maintained in the collective mind of the rabbinate. Without these presuppositions, the entire enterprise of responsa writing is a meaningless exercise. As the very content of the **Rabbinische Gutachten** shows, however, these very presuppositions are what are under attack, and so the use of the responsa-form is at some level self-contradictory. Let me show you what I mean.

Aaron Chorin, one of the earliest rabbis to publicly support Reform, states matters succinctly. Citing **Sifre**, he claims that the Jew's obligation is to follow the authorities of his generation, even if these teach that left is right and right is left. They, he goes on to say, have the same authority as Moses did in his time. (19) The implications of this are, of course, breathtaking. If the current rabbinic establishment has the authority of Moses, then the citation of earlier material is useless. The authority of the current rabbinate is self-standing and ultimate. As Chorin puts it, "The divine man Moses ... has according to the above-cited principle established a model for legislation which following legal tribunals should imitate. (20) The logic sounds like that of Clarence Darrow in **Inherit the Wind**. If Moses did not cite earlier authorities, why should we?

Other writers in the volume make what is essentially the same point although in less radical a fashion. Dr. Hess, Landrabbiner of the Grand Duchy of Weimar, compares Geiger to the great rabbis of the **Talmud**, an equal to Saadiah Gaon and Maimonides. (21) All of these men could differ with the accepted practice if their understanding of Judaism so dictated. Geiger then, has at least as much right to do so. His view can stand on his rabbinic office alone, regardless of what others hold or have held. We might, in this light, read the statement of Samuel Holdheim in Schwerin who states that Geiger has not mocked the **Talmud** but has in fact "dealt with the **Talmud** scientifically and with religious seriousness ....". (22) The use of the word "scientifically" here is significant. It means that Geiger wants to understand the rabbinic tradition in light of modern philosophical and historical methodologies. The application of Judaic wisdom and lore to the modern would must be put on a rational, enlightened, that is, **Wissenschaftlich** basis. The older rabbinic ways of thinking will no longer do. It thus follows that citing older rabbinic writings, or at least invoking the mainstream of classical scholarship, is at best besides the point. Geiger and the other "scientific" rabbis stand not only on a par with the authority of older rabbis, but are in fact to be preferred today because of the up-to-date nature of their methodology. So again, why prove their point by invoking past interpretations? The point in all this is to show that the authority claimed for Geiger is of such a kind that the whole need to use the responsa format at all is undercut. It becomes an empty form. It is no wonder that in German Reform as it was now being articulated, the struggle to appropriate the responsa form fizzled out.

We now turn to America and what I have called the third era in Reform responsa-writing. On this side of the Atlantic the story was quite different, for reasons I will adduce in due course. What can be said at the outset is that the responsa form not only was planted in the soil of the New World, but took root and flourished. As interesting as it is to know why responsa died in Germany Reform, it is just as interesting to know why they flourished here.

It must be borne in mind that there was a considerable hiatus between the last **Gutachten** of German Reform and the first publication of American Reform responsa. This is due in part to the late start American Reform Judaism had in becoming organized. It is possible, if one is looking for firm dates, to say Reform began here in 1838 with the introduction of an organ into the worship service of Congregation Beth El in Charleston, South Carolina. The organ was, of course, a prime symptom of reforming tendencies. But it was really only after the Civil Was that American Reform began to achieve stable institutional expression. The Union of American Hebrew Congregations was established by Isaac M. Wise in 1873. Two years later the Hebrew Union College formally opened. In 1889, the first alumni of the College came together to form the Central Conference of American Rabbis. It was this later group that organized the first "official" responsa writing authority for Reform Judaism in America. This is nearly fifth years after the publication of the two **Gutachten** volumes mentioned above.

We should pause for a moment to consider the implications of the above statement. It is noteworthy that responsa-writing in America was not left up to individual authorities, as was the custom in traditional Judaism for the past millennium. Responsa in America were to be the authorized expression of a rabbinic conference. This is really a throwback to the original character of responsa as the genre emerged during Gaonic times.

These early responsa, we recall, conveyed to the questioner the considered opinion of the Talmudic academy. The American movement now replicates the process, with responsa bearing the imprimatur not of an individual authority, but of the collective body of American (Reform) rabbis. It is this shift from individual to communal authorship which may help account for the acceptance of responsa in the New World.

It must be said that the idea of responsa writing in America had a slow and tentative start. It was really not until the 1950's that American Reform responsa became a clearly established aspect of the movement. What I want to do now is examine the roots and early history of American Reform responsa in preparation for our consideration of Reform responsa today.

As I mentioned, the CCAR had its beginning in 1889. It was not until 1907. however, that a Responsa Committee is listed as part of the structure of the CCAR. As far as I can tell, its first published responsum appeared in the **CCAR Yearbook** in 1913. Even then, however, the committee's work was far from accepted. In 1915, Rabbi Lauterbach complained that, "In a report of this character, the authority should be given for every decision so that the younger rabbis may see the development of the ideas involved. The answer should show on what basis the responsa were given". (23) Apparently like early Gaonic responsa, the committee simply issued a resolution without accompanying argumentation explaining why it ruled as it did. This alone shows us that the Committee understood itself to be dealing with a rather different order of responsa than the classical rabbinic model. Not only were the answers thin, however, but so was business. The following year, 1916, the chair of the Responsa Committee complained, "As chairman of the Committee on Responsa, I have all these years written a report of the Responsa Committee without receiving regular **sheelot**, except perhaps one or two that came in at the last moment". (24) The beginnings of responsa-writing in American Reform do not appear auspicious.

It is rather interesting to review the products of the CCAR's Responsa Committee during its early years. The first chair, Kaufman Kohler, would, of course, have a major influence on the future development of the American Reform responsa tradition since he in essence invented it. For this task, he was well suited. Kohler grew up in Fuerth, Bavaria, which had earned a reputation for being a center of rabbinic learning, and began his rabbinic studies there. Later, he moved to Frankfort where he came under the influence of the chief thinker of German neo-Orthodoxy, Samson Raphael Hirsch. Subsequently, Kohler became engaged in secular, university study, earning a degree from Erlangen in 1867. (25) The result was that the creator of the American Reform responsa tradition had both a good grounding in rabbinic and neo-Orthodoxy and a solid university education.

The influence of both aspects appear in his writings, thereby introducing a sort of ambivalence into the character of American Reform responsa. At times, Kohler draws on classical rabbinic literature in a way reminiscent of any traditional rabbi. More often, however, his responsa read more like academic essays on the history of Jewish religion and customs. Good examples are afforded by two of the first responsa he published, both in the **Yearbook** Vol XXIII (1913). (26) The one has to do with whether or not the weekly **Torah** portion should be read in English. Kohler's answer, reflecting his rabbinic background, is that the portion should first of all be read in Hebrew. After that, it would certainly be appropriate to translate that into the vernacular, following the example of the classical **meturgeman**. In that same issue, Kohler is asked about the **Bar Mitzvah** ceremony. Here we see emerge his secular, academic side. For Kohler, this ceremony is nothing more than a survival of "orientalism" with no worth now-a-days. It should, in his view, be replaced with the Confirmation ceremony. Thus the champion of **Torah** reading in Hebrew can, in the next breath as it were, dismiss the **Bar Mitzvah** ceremony, centered on the **Torah** reading, as unneeded. We see the same ambivalence the next year. (27) To a question concerning whether or not one may make distinctions among the dead Kohler responds simply that the question is easily solved and refers the reader to the **Shulkhan Arukh** Yoreh Deah Hil. Avelut; an answer worthy of any Orthodox rabbi. The next question concerns the observance of **Yahrzeit**. Now Kohler's answer is that the custom should be maintained not on the basis of custom or **Shulkhan Arukh**, but because of its educational value!

The character of the responsa written under

Kohler's watch were, of course, influenced, at least in part, by the questions to which he was asked to respond. The bulk of the questions put to him from 193 to 1922 dealt with various aspects of marriage and burials. In these areas there were a number of customs and folkways that seriously concerned people and that stood in stark contrast to Western practice. In a sense Kohler was forced either to tell people that a certain practice was mandated by rabbinic tradition and teaching, or to exercise his historical-critical faculty and reassure people that the old, embarrassing folkways taught by grandfather could safely be ignored. There was, in a word, little truly **halakhic** material that would allow him to exercise the responsa form in its classical sense.

On the other hand, when truly **halakhic** questions did appear before the Responsa Committee, it often failed to respond adequately. Let me give just two examples. In his report in vol XXVII (1918), Kohler reports on a question put to him about a child born apparently already circumcised. (28)

After examination, the **mohel** said nothing further needed to be done. The question was whether or not it would be permitted in this case to go ahead and name the baby without **b'rit milah**. Kohler apparently sick in bed, simply wired back his affirmative answer. (29) He was subsequently criticized on the grounds that he should have required at least **tipat dam**, a symbolic re-circumcision. Here was a good chance for Kohler to write a solid classical responsum, and he allowed the opportunity to slip by. A similar situation appears in vol. XXIX (1919). (30) The question was whether or not Pyrex could be considered glass such that if it had once been used to cook meat, it could subsequently be used to cook dairy products. The responsum, published over the name of Gotthardt Deutsch, treated the question as trivial, and contained an answer that was neither well-thought out nor well argued. Apparently these type of Orthodox-sounding questions did not engage the interest or intellect of these early Reform **posqim**. As a contrast you might consider the report of the committee the following year (1920) on what Jewish liturgical ceremonies (**qiddush**, wedding, Passover seder, etc) required the use of wine. Asked in the wake of the adoption of the 18th amendment, this responsum consumed nearly five pages of close argumentation and analysis. (31) Serious and detailed responsa could be written when the Committee felt the urge.

I cite these numerous cases to make a simple point. The first generation of American Reform responsa were interested in only a certain range of issues. As Kohler himself put it in 1913, "To sum up all I have said, we must in all matters of reform and progress agree upon the leading **principles** and not allow them to become arbitrary and individualistic....". (32) He was interested in scholarly essays which would examine the history of Jewish culture to determine what was essential for today's world. These issues engaged him; merely **halakhic** trivialities did not. This is indicated not only by what was and was not asked, but also by how the occasional **halakhic** questions that did emerge were handled.

Along these same lines, it must be pointed out that other presumably **halakhic** issues were being considered by the Conference at this time, but not in the context of the Responsa Committee. Conference Committees were working at this same time on the question of music in the liturgy, on writing a new prayerbook, on revising the **Pesah**

Haggadah, on determining responsibility for social action, on considering services held during the summer months, and on composing a "minister's handbook" which would establish a Reform standard in baby-namings, conversions, marriages, funerals and the like. The Responsa Committee worked in the interstices.

All in all then, we can say that Responsa writing as a function of the CCAR started late, had a rough beginning and continued to be a sort of step-child. Under Kohler's midwifery, Reform responsa came to be reminiscent of the Gaonic responsa. They were the decisions, sometimes oracular, of the collective body of rabbinic leaders, represented in this case not by the dean of the academy but by the chair of the Responsa Committee. It was also the case that the main focus would be on matters of principle, not on actual **halakhic** development. In short, Reform responsa in America addressed practical needs in a form that was in essence an academic essay. The rabbinic learning evident in them was rarely to the level we would expect of the men whose signature they bore.

Despite, or maybe because of, these characteristics, the enterprise of writing responsa for the American Reform Jewish community continued. The effort had clear institutional support from the CCAR itself. The committee continued to function and had as its chair some of the most distinguished scholars that the Reform movement had to offer:Kaufmann Kohler (who was also president of Hebrew Union College, thus making the connection between his responsa and the Gaonic responsa even more striking). Jacob Lauterbach (1923 to 1933), Jacob Mann (1934-1939), and then Israel Bettan (1940 to 1954). (33) Support on the part of the broad membership of the Conference, however, was another matter. Through the late twenties, and all of the thirties and forties, the publication of responsa in the **Yearbook** was spotty at best. In some years the Committee had no recorded report at all. At other times its report consisted of little more than an announcement that only a few questions had arrived and had been answered directly by the chair. Only every two or three years, on the average, did the committee feel it worthwhile to publish one or more of its responsa as being of more general interest. So the Committee continued to exist, to be led by prestigious scholars, but to be something of a sideshow.

Even a cursory look through the Tables of Contents of the **Yearbooks** reveals that a change wa starting to take form in the early fifties. One harbinger of this was the commission given to the committee in 1950 to bear primary responsibility for drafting a paper which would express the Conference's support a bill in the New York state assembly that would legalize euthanasia in certain cases. The lengthy result, published in the **Yearbook** for 1950, thrust the Committee into a prominence it had never had before. (34) In fact, it had published hardly anything for the last decade. The clouds of change gathered even more ominously by 1952, when the **Yearbook** published two responsa (the last time that happened was 1941), the first of which contained two answers, the one by Alexander Guttmann being a model of classical rabbinic scholarship complete with the citation of sources in Hebrew. The storm burst in 1953, with five responsa published, and thereafter there was a steady and unbroken drizzle of reponsa (if I may belabor the metaphor just a bit). From 1952 on, then, responsa are a fixture in the **Yearbook**.

This year was significant in other regards as well. It was at just this time that responsa began to appear in the new professional journal published by the CCAR. (35) Responsa were moving from being occasional committee reports to being part of the fare of Reform rabbinic professional reading. It was also at about this time that the Committee chair passed to Dr. Solomon Freehof. For all these reasons, then, I think we are justified in saying that the early 1950's marks a turning point in the evolution of American Reform responsa-writing. To understand what changed and what that change might mean, we need to turn to the formal characteristics of these new-age responsa. It is to this task that we now turn.

We can sum up at least the gross formal characteristics of Reform responsa since the mid-fifties under four topics. First of all, under Freehof we see emerging the Reform equivalent, for the first time, of a **poseq**, that is, a rabbi who emerges as a responsa authority on the basis of his own personal qualifications, not only as the holder of an office. Second, there is an almost exponential increase in the number of Reform **sheelot** submitted and so in the number and themes of the resulting responsa. This is illustrated simply by the number of collections of responsa published by Dr. Freehof over the past thirty years or so: **Reform Responsa** (1960), **Recent Reform Responsa** (1963), **Current Reform Responsa** (1969),**Modern Reform Responsa** (1971). **Contemporary Reform Rsponsa** (1974), **Reform Responsa for Our Time** (1977) and **New Reform Responsa** (1980). In all, there is now a veritable library of Reform responsa on library shelves, dealing with a broad range of issues.

This is a far cry from the early years in which responsa of the Reform movement were found only buried in the Responsa Committee reports of the CCAR, and then only every second or third year. So we have the first two characteristics of Reform responsa today, the emergence of the Reform equivalent of a **poseq** and the corresponding creating of a publically accessible Reform responsal literature covering literally hundreds of questions.

Two more formal characteristics of contemporary Reform responsal writing should be mentioned, both pointing to a reconception within the movement of the nature of responsa-literature for the Reform movement. The one, the third of the four we promised, has to do with how the responsa argue their case. In general, the first generation of Reform responsa tended to base their argument - when they had one - around what were assumed to be universally accepted philosophical and religious truths. This is, of course, perfectly predictable on the basis of the Reform movement's European roots in German idealism. For both Kant and Hegel, the two great philosophers on whom the Reform movement drew for its intellectual self-understanding, the concrete aspects of a religious life were but reflections of the more abstract reality of the cosmos. When remaking a religious tradition, as the German reformers were doing, one turned not to the tradition itself, but to the truths of the cosmos that philosophical inquiry revealed. That is why, it seems to me, that early rabbinic **teshuvot**. This influence also carried over in the early responsa of the CCAR. As writers on Reform Jewish practice, they saw themselves more as Jewish interpreters of philosophical and religious truths than as continuators of rabbinic culture. This is why they rarely cited earlier rabbinic sources, and when they did it was likely to be Maimonides, a fellow philosopher.

This dependence on the German idealistic philosophical tradition is no longer so evident in Freehof. His tactic, certainly rhetorically but also substantively, is to go back to classical rabbinic responsa and adduce a Reform position from them. That is, Freehof's responsa present themselves as continuous not with Kant or Hegel, but with the responsa literature in general. His texts are certainly Reform in spirit, but reading them is reminiscent of reading traditional rabbinic texts once again.

We might wish briefly to speculate on the meaning of this shift. It is, of course, the case that American Reform Judaism is a different movement from German Reform. While this is self-evident, it probably does not hurt to say this occasionally. Freehof reflects in his essence the American situation, not the European one. Second, his retrieval of a virtual library of responsa material from post-Holocaust Europe provided a corpus of resources. Third, we might point to the gradual reappropriation of tradition by Reform in the post-Holocaust period. To put matters somewhat bluntly, it seemed now more appropriate to base Reform ethics on medieval rabbis than on a modern German philosopher. These reasons, among others, provide the cultural background within which Solomon Freehof's unique intellectual gifts could be applied to, of (all) things, Reform responsa.

I said earlier that there were four formal characteristics of contemporary Reform responsa that I wished briefly to present. We have now mentioned three: Freehof as Reform **poseq**, the exponential increase in **sheelot** and so of Reform responsa, and the reappropriation of traditional rabbinic writings into the argument. The fourth characteristic, which I take as significant, is the publication of **Responsa of the C.C.A.R.** in 1954 and more recently of Walter Jacob's collection of past responsa of the CCAR in his **American Reform Responsa**. (36) I think these are significant because they reflect a willingness on the part of American Reform to acknowledge, preserve and make accessible its own response tradition. It signals, I believe the acceptance of writing responsa into American Reform Judaism. These collections indicate that writing responsa is now an accepted, long-standing and important part of American liberal Judaism.

Let me sum up my argument so far. We have now seen the outstanding features of Reform responsa from the publication of **Noga Hatzedeq** to the present day. Our review has revealed both successes and failures. We have seen the formally Orthodox material in **Noga Hatzedeq** prove to be sterile within Reform Judaism. At the same time we saw that the "**Gutachten**" -genre also failed to seen an ongoing literary tradition. On the other hand, the American style of responsa has proven to be vital and fecund. Since the point of this study is to learn about the nature of Reform **halakhah**, and we have chosen to do so through an examination of its characteristic literature, responsa, we must now try to draw some lessons from the evidence before us.

I think we can account for the failures of the German Reform responsa fairly easily. The **Noga Hatzedeq** style failed to catch because, as I said, it was too bound up with the contemporary Orthodox mode of responsa-writing, and so depended too heavily on the presuppositions that made Orthodox responsa work, presuppositions that the Reform movement was specifically dedicated to denying. The **Gutachten** on the other hand were too secular to justify themselves as Judaic literature. Given their rhetoric, one wonders why simple academic journal articles wold not work as well. In fact such journal essays did become the primary vehicle for the expression and development of subsequent German Reform. In short both forms failed for the same reason, neither type developed a format that was able to synthesize traditional Judaic rhetorical form with contemporary religious content. Each settled on an extreme. This conclusion suggests what it was about the discourse found in the American responsa that allowed this mode to succeed. It shaped a rhetoric reminiscent of classical Judaic discourse that was nonetheless compatible with modern religious needs.

Before concluding, let me speculate briefly on the dynamic apparent in the development of American Reform responsa. In the early part of this paper, I compared the first generation of American Reform responsa to the responsa of the Gaonim, the heads of the Talmudic academies in Babylonia in the ninth and tenth centuries. At that time I pointed out as basic characteristics shared by both the general brevity of the responsa, the citation of little else than Scripture and maybe **Talmud** - that is, the most basic sources - and the claim to authority based on the office of the signee (Gaon, chair of the Responsa Committee). I now want to argue that what we see emerging in subsequent Reform responsa-those published from the early 1950's on-correspond in suggestive ways to the phase in the development of the classical responsa tradition that followed the Gaonic period. By the tenth or early eleventh century, as I said, the Gaonic academies in Babylonia were in decline. In their place there emerged a number of new rabbinic centers in the car-flung corners of the Jewish world, in North

Africa, for example, and in southern Europe. Responsa came to be written more and more by local, individual **posqim**, decisors who had earned for themselves a reputation for scholarship. These **posqim** could not rely on their office itself to impart authority to their responsa, and so they resorted to argumentation, especially argumentation based on past authority, whether Scripture, **Talmud** or eventually even other responsa. Their rulings were no longer simply declared, but rather adduced. They had to be made credible in the marketplace of ideas. Further, since, these were local authorities living and working amid Jews in the newly emerging culture of Europe, responsa began to take on a much wider range of issues. Finally, there is good evidence to suggest that it was at this time, the eleventh through fourteenth centuries, that European rabbis first began seriously to collect and preserve the responsa of the Gaonic past. The reason was, no doubt, because these now became precious resources for the creation of new responsa. All in all, with the collection of older responsa, the emergence of individual rabbinic **posqim** and the increasing area of responsa concern, we can say that responsa in the 10th through 12th centuries became rabbinized.

The parallels with what appears to be happening with Reform responsa are interesting. We see a similar maturation, a sort of Reform-rabbinization, occurring within our own tradition. First of all the responsa have grown from being short and at times cursory proclamations of the Responsa Committee, to fully developed essays which argue their point in detail and tie their results closely to rabbinic sources. Second, the range of literature cited has become wider. With Dr. Freehof, for the first time classical rabbinic responsa are routinely cited along with the old standbys of Scripture, **Talmud** and **Shulkhan Arukh**. Third, again with Dr. Freehof, the person who issues the responsa begins to have an authority based on his own scholarship, not merely as the holder of an official position. And we also have the collection and republication of older responsa. We seem, in short, to be witnessing a recapitulation of the development of the responsa literature within our own movement. Needless to say, this has tremendously interesting implications for what Reform is, how it relates to traditional rabbinism, and for what its future trajectory might be. These speculations, however, move us into the future and so into another paper.

We may, however, ask what all this means for our understanding of Reform **halakhah**. Although our historical perspective is short - Reform is only about a century and a half old, and Reform responsa barely eighty years - nonetheless I think some tentative conclusions can be ventured. First of all, the success of responsa in America tells us, I think, that such a thing as Reform **halakhah** is emerging. The word **halakhah** clearly has a different meaning in Reform than it does in Orthodoxy, but when a responsa-type literature can be sustained for eighty years, some concept of **halakhah** must be at work. I think further that if the analogy which I have drawn between the trajectory of Reform responsa and that of the Gaonic/early medieval responsa is correct, then we will see Reform **halakhah** becoming both more pervasive and more decentralized as time passes. More and more issues will come up for Reform **halakhic** scrutiny and more and more Reform rabbis will become involved in writing responsa to deal with them. Further, if the analogy holds, Reform practice will become not less diverse, but more so. What will hold matters together is not so much a common **minhag**, but a common sense that whatever we do must be grounded in the literature of our common heritage, just as was true in the early Middle Ages.

It is, of course, the notion that a concept of Reform **halakhah** is beginning to manifest itself in our movement that is so interesting. I think this represents an important stage in the re-rabbinization of Reform. The Reform movement began as a lay movement that was soon explicitly rejecting traditional rabbinic authority, as were other modernist movements such as Hassidism two generations earlier and as Zionism would two generations later. It gathered rabbinic support only gradually and has still not fully done so. But even the rabbis who gradually came to lead the movement in Germany in the 1830's and 1840's were hardly rabbinical in the classical sense. They were more modern academicians than anything else. In fact, by the late nineteenth century, German Reform was still presenting itself as a kind of universal religion of reason, completely pushing aside its particularistic roots. The movement, especially in ethnic-conscious America has turned back the other way. There is among us a strong sense of ethnic identity, of a common history and heritage, and a commitment to take charge of our own particular destiny as a people. In this change, Reform has slowly become re-rabbinized in the sense that it is turning away from reliance on secular philosophy and turning toward its indigenous spiritual authority centered in the rabbinic office. This development, I submit, is evidenced in the new flourishing of Reform responsa, a literature which draws its lifeblood from the values, principles and rhetoric of the rabbinic estate. What is emerging, of course, in not the classical rabbinic responsa of Orthodoxy. We are in the process of creating our own modern rabbinic culture. In this process of birth, the tradition of Reform responsa writing plays a subtle, but I think also essential, role. If so, then Solomon Freehof and Walter Jacob have played midwife to a major process of revitalization in American Reform Judaism.

Notes

1. Jakob Petuchowski, **Prayerbook Reform in Europe, the Liturgy of European Liberal and Reform Judaism**, New York, WUPJ, 1968, esp. chap. 5.

2. Published in Hamburg by B. S. Berendsohn, 1842.

3. Published in Breslau by Leopold Freund, 1943.

4. The Committees first appearance occurs in vol. XXI 1911, p. 67, but is simply recorded as an oral report received by the Conference. The first published text I could find is in vol. XXIII, 1913, pp. 166ff.

5. **American Reform Responsa: Collected Responsa of the Central Conference of American Rabbis**, 1889-1983, ed. by Walter Jacob, New York, CCAR, 1983.

6. A resolution was presented during the 1906 Conference calling on the president "to appoint a committee of two to whom such questions may be submitted and who shall furnish the responsa for the Year Book" vol. XVI, 1906, p. 67. There is no record of the approval of this resolution by the Resolution Committee. However, the next volume of the **Year Book** lists an eight member Responsa Committee for 1907-1908.

7. See especially Joel Mueller, "Brief und Responsen in der vorgeonaeischen juedischen Literatur" **Vierter Bericht ueber die Lehranstahlt fuer die Wissenschaft des Judenthums**, Berlin, 1866, pp. 3-4.

8. The exact date when responsa began to be written is still unclear. See Simha Assaf in

"Techuvot Hagaonim" in **Tekufat HaGeonim Vesifrutam**, Jerusalem, Mossad HaRav Kook, 1967, p. 21.

9. A detailed reconstruction of how the Gaonic office worked is Alexander D. Good, "The Exiarchate in the Eastern Caliphate, 637-1258" in **Jewish Quarterly Review, New Series, vol.** 31, 1940-41, pp. 149-169. See also Salo Baron, **A Social and Religious History of the Jews** New York, Columbia, 1957- , vol. V, pp. 5-24. Simha Assaf tries to suggest how questions were received and answers sent in **"Ha'im Katvu Hagaonim et Teshuvotehem raq bekalah Beadar?"** in **Tekufot**, pp. 257-260.

10. The decline of the Gaonate is described in Simha Assaf and Joshua Brand, "Gaon" in **Encyclopedia Judaica**, VII, 318. See also Jacob Mann, **Texts and Studies II**, Philadelphia, JPS, 1935, pp. 202f. The rise of local rabbinic centers especially in Spain and North Africa is detailed in Eliyahu Ashtor, **The Jews of Moslem Spain**, trans. by Aaron Klein and Jenny M. Klein, Philadelphia, 1973, I, pp. 230-241. For southern Europe and developments, cf. Cecil Roth, "Introduction", **The World History of the Jewish People**, XI, Rutgers, 1966, p.6.

11. The intellectual background to this development is presented by Isidore Fishman, **The History of Jewish Education in Central Europe**, London, Goldstar, 1944, especially pp. 103-109.

12. **Noga Hatzedeq** Dessau, G. Schlieder, 1818, p. 19. Actually, this volume contains a number of different responsa, including **Derekh Haqodesh** by ShemTov ben Joseph Chaim ben Samon, **Ya'ir Nativ** by Jacob Chai Reconati; **Kenat Haemet** by Aaron Chaim and an essay, **Or Nogah,** by Eliezer Libermann. Selections from all of these are translated by Alexander Guttmann in **The Struggle over Reform in Rabbinic Literature**, New York, WUPJ, 1977, pp. 177-208.

13. The text of the ban is reprinted in the

introduction to this volume, pp. 14-15.

14. **Theologische Gutachten,** p. 109. This same point, using similar language is made in the **Talmud of the Land of Israel**, Yoma 39:2 and Yebamot 12:1, for example.

15. **Ibid.**, p. 36.

16. **Ibid.**, p. 78.

17. Solomon A. Tiktin, **Darstellung des Sachverhaeltnissess in seiner hiesigen Rabbinate-Angelegenheit,** Breslau, H. Richter, 1842. A general introduction to the debate with a translation of some of the texts may be found in W. Gunther Plaut, **The Rise of Reform Judaism,** New York, WUPJ, 1963.

18. See especially the opening piece by Friedlaender.

19. **Rabbinische Gutachten**, pp. 21-22, repeated on p.32.

20. **Ibid.**, p. 24

21. **Ibid.**, p. 151

22. **Ibid.**, p. 82.

23. **Yearbook of the CCAR**, V. XXV, 1915, p. 81.

24. **Ibid.**, V. XXVI, 1916, p.133.

25. **Encyclopedia Judaica,** X, p.1142.

26. The Responsa Committee report begins on p. 166.

27. **Yearbook,** V. XXIV, 1914, pp. 152-154.

28. **Yearbook,** V. XXVIII, 1918, pp. 117f.

29. The reference to his being sick appears as the beginning of his committee report as recorded in the **Yearbook**, V. XXXIX, 1919, p. 74. At this time he introduced a written supplement to his responsum of the previous year addressing the issue of **tipat dam**. This supplement appears on pp. 86-87 of the **Yearbook**

30. **Yearbook,** p. 79.

31. **Yearbook,** V. XXX, 1930, pp. 108-112.

32. **Yearbook**, V. XXIII, 1913, p. 183, emphasis in original.

33. Jacob Lauterbach was ordained by the

Rabbiner Seminar fuer Orthodoxes Judenthum, founded by Rabbi Azriel Hildesheimer. He thus had a solid foundation in Talmudic and rabbinic learning. His successor, Jacob Mann had a traditional Jewish education in his hometown of Przemysl, Galacia and later studied rabbinics at Jews' College in London. The fourth chair, Israel Bettan, was an ordainee of HUC. In his youth, however, he came to America at age 18, he studied in the renowned Slabodka Yeshiva.

34. **Yearbook**, V. LX 1950, pp. 107-110.

35. The **CCAR Journal** began to appear in 1953. Its first issue contains a responsum by Israel Bettan.

36. Walter Jacob, **American Reform Responsa**, New York, CCAR, 1983.

Chapter III

Philosopher and **Poseq**
Some Views of Modern Jewish Law

Walter Jacob

The Reform Movement and later its Conservative offshoot began as a gradual rebellion against Orthodoxy which was fearful of modern times. This meant that the evolutionary process and change which had been part of Judaism since its beginning were suddenly no longer possible. For example, Biblical translations have an ancient history in Judaism going back twenty-five hundred years, but despite that Moses Mendelssohn's translation was banned by a number of traditional authorities mainly on the grounds that his work would serve as an introduction to modern German and its culture. Those who read it or made the attempt would spend more time studying German than the contents of the Pentateuch. It was naive to believe that banning such a work would solve the problem of the cultural clash. (1) The revolution was primarily practical in tone. It sought reforms in worship, education and daily practices. A generation passed before more theoretical basis was sought for the changes in Judaism. The initial effort by the liberal Jewish scholars of the second generation lay in the direction of finding a rationale for their form of Judaism in the past. They therefore, concerned themselves largely with history. So, Leopold Zunz, Abraham Geiger, Zacharias Frankel, Leopold Loew and others sought a historic basis for their liberal approach. At the same time, broader histories began to appear under the aegis of Michael Jost and Heinrich Graetz. This historical approach seemed appropriate and satisfying, especially in an age which was noted for a broad general interest in history and a re-examination of its underlying principles.

This did not mean that philosophy and theology were entirely neglected, but they certainly played a secondary role in the early Reform Movement. The system of thought created by Moses Mendelssohn hardly survived him as the basis on which it had been built was destroyed by Emanuel Kant. In the nineteenth century a number of other philosophers dominated Jewish and general thought; leading among them were Hegel, Fichte, and Schleiermacher. Several liberal Jewish thinkers adapted their philosophical approaches to Judaism and modified them appropriately. Except for the work of Herman Cohen at the end of the century, none of these efforts had any broader impact and their influence was restricted to a relatively narrow academic circle. Among these thinkers were Samuel Hirsch, Salomon Formstecher and Salomon Steinheim. None of these individuals concerned themselves deeply with the place of **halakhah** as there were other issues which they deemed more pressing and to which they turned their attention.

The pattern followed in the United States was rather similar. The early generation of reformers both lay and rabbinic turned their attention to practical matters, so an educational system was created, prayerbooks were written, newspapers founded, and congregations were formed. Isaac Mayer Wise, the creator of the organizations of Reform Judaism, expressed himself on virtually every issue of the times, but his writings on **halakhah** are minimal. His personal approach was quite traditional and he was willing to make the rabbinic tradition the basis of a national Jewish organization in 1855. David Einhorn, on the other hand, was far more radical, but also had relatively little to say about **halakhah** in any systematic form. The theologians of Reform Judaism, Kaufman Kohler, and his disciple Samuel Cohon, dealt with **halakhah**, and provided a theoretical important place for it, but then left its status undefined. Kaufman Kohler, for example, was proposed a radical statement on the rabbinic past as part of the Pittsburg Platform (#3 and #4), but at the same time maintained a much more traditional approach in the catechism written for his congregation. Furthermore the other items of the agenda of the Pittsburgh Rabbinic Conference were all discussed within the framework of rabbinic Judaism. (2) Later he was quite willing to accept the appointment as Chairman of the Responsa Committee when it was established in 1907; it had been organized at his suggestion. The early responsa which Kohler wrote were naturally based on the rabbinic tradition and the fact that they were issued at all indicated an interest in **halakhah**.

If we turn to Solomon Schechter, the founder of the organized Conservative Movement in the United States, we find that he was principally interested in the historical approach to Judaism. The volumes of his essays contain lovely pieces on the past, but certainly no well thought out effort in the direction of **taamei mitzvot**. It was left for the next generation of Conservative Jews to move in a different direction.

Only in this century has more systematic approach to the **halakhah** and its rationale been on the Liberal Jewish agenda. The Liberal Jewish movement with its Reform and Conservative wings has both turned to **halakhah** and to a rationale for it. Both groups have continued the age old effort of adapting Judaism to a new culture, a task which has a long and honored history among us.

Mitzvot were observed, but their rationale questioned. There was intense debate about what was actually required and early rabbinic debates were reopened. At times those who discussed the details of the **mitzvot** also provided a rationale for them. That was not necessarily so. In the Middle Ages the Jewish thinkers most involved in the **mitzvot** themselves were sometimes also the philosophers who provided a rationale. Saadia and Maimonides, as well as a few others among the Sephardim followed this route. More often, the philosopher and the **poseq** went down different roads and were not particularly concerned with each other's efforts. This has been equally true in modern times. At the beginning of the modern period, Moses Mendelssohn sought an entirely new approach to **halakhah** from a philosophical point of view, but was not particularly concerned with the detailed exposition of the **mitzvot** in the form of responsa or codes. Perhaps the only exception in the last century to this rule was the Orthodox Samson Raphael Hirsch who sought to provide both an Orthodox rationale and dealt with the system of observance in his various works, sometimes not consistent with his Orthodoxy, (3) however, we will not deal with the figures of the last century, but turn to a selection of those who made their leading contributions in the twentieth century or whose influence has been felt primarily in our century. We realize that both roads are of vital importance for the modern Jew who needs to find some spiritual moorings. We might expect the modern westernized Jew to place more emphasis on the rationale of the commandments and less on the details of observance, that actually is not so.

Therefore, both areas continue to evolve in their separate ways and one might say in search of an individual who can present a unified theory of observance along with a practical expression of it. This paper will attempt to see where we stand rather than seek new avenues.

Some of the individuals who were leaders among liberal Jews might have been expected to present a rationale for the commandments. They did not. So, for example, Leo Baeck (1873-1959), the last great liberal rabbi of Germany who stayed behind with his community as its national president, wrote many scholarly essays, but his emphasis was more on **midrash** and **agadah** than on **halakhah**. His essay, "Mysticism and the Commandments" in **Judaism and Christianity**, really dealt more with the phenomenon of mysticism than with **halakhah**. Leo Baeck considered **halakhah** as only "one constituent part of the divine revelation", (4) although personally observant in a liberal manner. **halakhah** did not possess the authority for him which it once had for traditional Jews. His last book, **This People, Israel**, was a kind of a **midrash** which hardly dealt with **halakhic** considerations at all.

Perhaps the most influential thinkers of twentieth century European Jewry were Martin Buber (1878-1965) and Franz Rosenzweig (1886-1929). Martin Buber's approach to **halakhah** can be read a number of different ways. He was accused of being antinomian. After all, the entire I-Thou system of philosophy depended upon a an existentialist approach to God and Judaism. This could occur entirely outside the **halakhic** system. For him it is not only the end result which may be doubtful when viewed through the eyes of

halakhah but also the path taken for the **halakhah** requires a fixed daily approach to God independent of any encounter between man and God. Critics have naturally pointed out that the latter may occur only rarely and so is an uncertain path toward a religious life. (5)

On the positive side, one may defend Buber's approach by stating that he wished to rescue **halakhah** from becoming merely ortho-practice. Buber wanted to infuse the law with the ancient spirit so that individuals would once more become responsible for their lives. (6) For him as he explained perhaps most thoroughly in his book, **Two Types of Faith**, the **halakhah** always had to be part of a demanding voice with a sense of highly personally responsibility. This voice addressed the individual and only in this way could the objective statement become a personal **mitzvah**.

The entire system, therefore, depended upon what Maurice Friedman has called, "Holy insecurity of the religious man who does not divorce his action from his intention." (7) The traditional approach demanded observance and provided security through that observance. The price that was paid was an automatic approach to **halakhah**. For Martin Buber the a genuine approach to God was frequently filled with tension and insecurity common to our century but the reward was through religiosity and the feeling of personal commitment.

For Martin Buber, in keeping with his I-Thou relationship, the emphasis of Sinai was less on commandment and more on covenant. The commandment was to prepare the people for the covenant. (8) The very nature of the words spoken at Sinai indicate this through the beginning of the Decalogue with "I," addressed to the "Thou", here the people of Israel. As there were no enforcing mechanisms mentioned the individual had the freedom to accept or reject the commandment or for that matter, the covenant. (9)

Perhaps Howard Simon (10) has put it very well when he stated that Buber saw the **halakhic** system as a kind of a merry-go-round continually circling. The individual Jew must decide to get on it or not. Where he does so is irrelevant. It must be done as a matter of personal decision, not automatically. Buber, therefore, placed his emphasis on an open spontaneous relationship between God and man and between man and God. If there is no immediacy about the experience, then it represents merely a part of the historic continuity of the Jewish people, but can mean nothing to the individual personally. **Halakhah**, therefore, remained in many ways unexplored terrain which the individual must explore for himself.

Franz Rosenzweig approached the matter somewhat differently and argued with Martin Buber for he felt that the individual was bound to follow the tradition although he might not accept all of it yet. The tradition may move the individual in the direction of a religious experience and therefore he would make **halakhah** part of his life while remaining uncertain about his ultimate commitment. For Franz Rosenzweig the system of **halakhah** needed to be viewed in a broad historical manner, not just the revelation at Sinai but the totality of the teaching of Judaism. (11) Twentieth century man must struggle and make the traditional statements into **mitzvot** again but the only way of doing so is through observance rather than through waiting for a proper relationship between man and God. In his essay "Relation and Law", (12) Franz Rosenzweig dealt with the law in a number of ways. For him it was a prerequisite of Israel as a chosen people. Divine revelation became something that human beings could understand and to which they could relate. The **halakhah** was less a statement of God than a "soliloquy" of human beings as they sought God. Rosenzweig was not so much concerned with the details of the law but with the spirit of sanctity which they had once provided for those who observed the. He like Buber opposed ortho-practice which led to blind unthinking observance. (13) As God's covenant with Israel was eternal it was necessary for each generation to transform the thoughts of that covenant to fit a new mood and a new era. That needed to be done through a process of change and selectivity. This was partially made on a highly personal basis and partially made by people as a whole. (14)

As both of of these thinkers were Existentialist philosophers, they began with the individual, however Buber carried the individualism much further and made that the primary criteria by which **halakhah** and **mitzvot** would be measured. Rosenzweig tried to create a synthesis of tradition with the Existentialist approach.

As we turn to America it may be well to begin with Abraham Heschel (1907-1972) who in some ways forms a bridge between Europe and America Heschel was educated in both the eastern and western European traditions and then spent the most signficant years of his teaching career in the United States. Heschel gave much of his creative effort to **halakhah** and the great **halakhic** thinkers of the past. His biography of Maimonides dealt with philosophical, mystical, as well as **halakhic** issues. His major work, **Torah Min Hashamayim** is a historical exploration of the entire realm of rabbinic literature. Abraham Heschel provided an insight into his personal understanding of the **mitzvah** through his essay. (15) There he explained how he began to feel a sense of "duty" to worship and to the other **mitzvot** while a student in Berlin. Although the university courses which he took emphasized symbolic thinking, this was not satisfactory for him as he felt that the **mitzvot** created orderly existence for each human being. (16) On a practical level he felt that modern man could not mechanically observe the **mitzvot** as that was of little purpose. He emphasized that there remained a vast gap between the all or nothing philosophy expressed by so many modern Jews. The real question was which segments of the **halakhah** can and should be fulfilled. (17) Modern man primarily sought for divine meaning in the **mitzvot** and was little concerned with their origin - a major concern in the nineteenth century. Heschel felt that the **mitzvot** would lead to meaning and that the modern Jew should not spend his time seeking a rationale for the commandments, "Its meaning must be understood in terms compatible with the sense of the ineffable". (18) He stressed the need for a 'leap of action', an approach very much in keeping with the traditional way of Judaism. For Abraham Heschel "the deed is the source of holiness." (19) The **mitzvot** represented the path to the sacred and within that path emphasis was to be placed upon **kavanah** rather than detailed observance. (20)

When Abraham Heschel turned to the details of the **halakhah** he strongly felt that there we were not dealing with divine commandments but human interpretations and that rabbinic authorities throughout the ages had made major changes. (21) So to him not all laws were equally significant; one could remove some of them without bringing the entire structure down. Man could approach God step by step and with single **mitzvot** without accepting the entire system. (22) Furthermore, the emphasis on all or nothing made the traditionalists, did not deal justly with the vast majority of modern Jews who had abandoned segments of Jewish life, but still considered themselves loyal Jews and were very much attached to Judaism. (23)

Heschel also made a clear division between commandments and customs or **minhagim**. As he felt that "Judaism does not stand on ceremonies.....Jewish piety is an answer to God expressed in the language of **mitzvot** rather than the language of ceremonies. The **mitzvah** rather than the ceremony is the fundamental category." (24) For Heschel ceremonies were folkways and not particular sacred while **mitzvot** represented the path of God or the interpretation of the will of God. This, of course, represented a vigorous disagreement with the approach of his colleague, Mordecai Kaplan, which will be discussed later. Ultimately when Heschel looked at the whole **halakhic** system he felt that it was only one component albeit a major one in man's attempt to reach out to God. For him the **agadah** was just as important as the **halakhah**. A Judaism limited solely to **halakhah** presented a distorted image of Judaism. (25) Perhaps it was put most beautifully in his summary: "**Halakhah** is the string; **agadah** is the bow. When the string is tight, the bow will evoke the melody." (26) It was perfectly possible for man to gradually climb up the ladder of spirituality step by step through observance of individual **mitzvot** and so come closer to God. This kind of approach overcame some of the criticism of those who felt that religious motivation through **kavanah** might be slow in coming and that a "leap of action" represented a path consistent with the traditions of Judaism.

Mordecai Kaplan (1881-1983), the founder and creator of Reconstructionist Judaism, slowly changed his approach to **halakhah** over the years. In his first work, **Judaism as a Civilization**, published in 1934, Kaplan vigorously attacked Reform, Conservative, and Orthodox Judaism, though in reality he was attacking what no longer existed as these branches of Judaism had changed by the mid-thirties.

In his effort to deal with **mitzvah** and **halakhah**, but without the inherited baggage attendant to these terms, Kaplan defined Jewish law as folkways. He never used the term **halakhah** for Jewish law and so gave it a personal definition which incorporated the legal and personal aspects of life along with communal piety and the emotional elements of religion which make it effective. Through his efforts, Kaplan wished to rescue and reconstitute as much of tradition as was possible for modern getimes. This was especially true of all those matters connected with the Jewish calendar or and the Jewish life-cycle. (27) This was likewise the pattern which he followed in his "Guide for Jewish Ritual Use" which appeared in the **Reconstructionist** in 1941. Through that effort he sought to give practical expression to theoretical framework provided in **Judaism as a Civilization**. In this work he expressed a broad tolerance for the wide spectrum of observance which existed in the American Jewish community. He felt that individual Jews should voluntarily associate themselves with whatever group met their specific needs. Within those groups the positive aspects of tradition rather than its prohibitions should be stressed. Kaplan also stressed that there should be a hierarchy of folkways so that not everything was on an equal level as is true in traditional Judaism. Most of all, his practical guide emphasized the need for the rediscovery of rituals and the need to infused new meaning in those which had lost their significance for modern people. As this was intended as a guide, Kaplan went into much practical detail in it. (28)

As Mordecai Kaplan proceeded to clarify his view of Judaism as a civilization, he incorporated **halakhah** as a major factor in that civilization. A fuller exposition of **halakhah** was provided in his book, **The Future of the American Jew** (1948). He faced the fact that ritual had been eliminated from the lives of many American Jews, particularly criticized traditional community for its exclusion of those who observed little of the **halakhah**. His broad view was that, "a religious civilization is one which not only identifies the individual with his group, but makes the group responsible for the salvation of the individual, for helping him to experience life is supremely worthwhile or holy and thus commune with God. A satisfactory rationale for Jewish usage is one that would recognize in it both a method of group survival and a means to the personal self-fulfillment, of salvation of the individual Jew." (29) Although guidance may be necessary Kaplan did not equate it with revealed codes. He felt strongly that the observances and symbols of the past had to play a major role, but they were to be viewed in precisely those sociological and historical terms. Whatever evolved the standards for folkways reflect individual as well as group wishes. Only two principles had to guide the group as it viewed its folkways: (a) survival as opposed to assimilation; (b) individual salvation which should add meaning to individual lives.

Kaplan felt that the community should set minimal standards and so differentiate between commandments not according to Biblical or rabbinic origins but according to their contemporary significance. They should be divided into three categories: (1) those which remain meaningful and form and content; (2) those which continue to be meaningful in content although the form may seem arbitrary and (3) those which are arbitrary in both form and content, but continue to possess meaning for a large number of Jews (dietary laws). All of these may ultimately be considered essential in one form or another, but they will also need adaptation and change to our specific age. Here Kaplan went considerably further than earlier. Whatever revisions and changes were made should be done in the spirit which was realistic and incorporated the democratic process. It was only in this way that the Jewish people could be reconstituted and that it may again express its will through the medium of law. (30) In any such revision of Jewish law, the age old principle of **dina d'malkhuta dina** would be given a new and much broader meaning. In any such recreated system, the community would have to create its own method of enforcement as divine sanctions had ceased to be effective. All would have to be established on a voluntary democratic basis. (31) Such procedures would be in keeping with the definition of God as "the power that makes for salvation" and democracy as the way in which the people move toward that salvation. Although Kaplan felt strongly that traditional law should continue to be observed and maintained whenever they continued to possess meaning and be reinterpreted when that meaning was gone, he also felt that new laws and rituals should be created when the need arose. Their acceptance might be slow but movement in this direction was necessary on a communal basis if the current chaos was to be overcome.

He felt that one of the primary difficulties in this entire effort was lay with both extremes, traditionalist on the one hand who saw meaning in every detail and a vast group at the other end of the spectrum who had never experienced any benefit from ritual, and so saw no value in it whatsoever. He felt that the only way to overcome this problem and to bridge the gap was through the creation of a large number of groups who would "formulate for themselves the criteria by which they will discriminate between observances that should be maintained, or, perhaps, that should be created and observances that ought to become obsolete." (32)

Kaplan felt strongly that much of this needs to be done not only in the Diaspora but also in Israel. Only in a democratic society would Jewish law again become significant. Furthermore, he indicated that frequently the Diaspora might serve as a role model for Israel. (33)

In various essays Kaplan also discussed

practical matters connected with **halakhah** such as the position of the **aguna**, the general role of women in Judaism, etc. He, therefore, because of his sociological approach was willing to deal with the actual details of the law as well as its broad theoretical structure.

In the contemporary Reform Jewish world, Eugene Borowitz (1925-) is without doubt the most significant theologian. His influence has been felt through his position as Professor of the Hebrew Union College - Institute of Religion (New York) and through his lively intellectual journal, **Sh'ma**, which has served as a forum for wide spectrum of American intellectual Jewish life. He has discussed **halakhah** and view of it in a number of books and essays. According to Borowitz, the principle problem which the modern Jew faces is the fact that there is no widely accepted philosophy upon which modern Jewish theology can be built. As as we live in an age of philosophical pluralism we can not duplicate the efforts of the Middle Ages which dealt with Neo-Platonic or Aristotilean thought. Nor can we properly follow the thinkers of the nineteenth century who were able to build on Kantian, Neo-Kantian or Hegelian philosophy, all of which were somewhat hospitable to religion. In contrast much of twentieth thought is hostile or neutral toward religion. In a society which is materialistic and utilitarian in its outlook theology finds itself in a difficult position. Yet, Eugene Borowitz is not willing to give up as he searches for "an antidote for paganism." That is not easy as the mood of universalism which provided such antidote in the past is now over. (34) For Borowitz we must begin from an extistentialist perspective and with the individual. Furthermore, he is much concerned with the autonomy and freedom of the individual. That becomes his overriding emphasis when dealing with **halakhah** and its traditions. It is the autonomous self which is most important for him. As the individual moves toward Judaism he "begins with God rather than **Torah**." (35) Borowitz has rejected God's revelation of the written and oral **Torah**, so we must ask what authority **Torah** and **halakhah** has for him and for us. In a highly structured essay presented to the Reform rabbinic conference, the best answer which presents a kind of universal ethics in which Jewish folkways and culture are the practical means of its execution. He would have the individual ask the question: "Is this an act I want to do for God; One I feel is appropriate to Him as best I have to know Him." (36) The commandment thus executed may stem from God, but it will be carried out because of the will of the individual. The individual must feel a sense of obligation whose source may be conscience, intuitive knowledge, or revelation. He also stressed the distinction between ethical commandments and rituals despite their occasional overlap and feels that it is the ethical prophetic statement which must always take precedence over ritual.

Borowitz is keenly aware of the problems which extreme individualism may bring and feels strongely that all Jews must be part of the community, but this needs to be brought about through the assent of the individual. It is only in this way that the individual can "help to redeem history." Although the individual can act religiously as an independent entity we would have to designate such individuals as "of Jewish descent, but not part of our people."

The border between the individual and the

community remains a rather gray area in Eugene Borowitz's thought for the final authority remains with the individual and "not in a book or code of the past." (37) Traditions and knowledge of the past, of course, help to establish present day norms and will guide individual, but they are not authoritative. The community may provide guidance and aid but in ultimately the individual or perhaps the family must make the decision. Yet the individual or family must also understand itself as part of a broader community if it wishes those decisions to be influential beyond the narrowest circle.

Borowitz felt strongly that the individual Reform Jew within the broader community should be creative and should form such new rituals as are an appropriate expression of the basic ethics and morality of Judaism and which will make them live in our time. This is especially important as no real American Jewish way of life has yet evolved and it is still being created.

As Borowitz looks at our broader influence on the stage of history he feels that all efforts to bring Israel and mankind closer to the Kingdom of God require covenant. It is the covenant which becomes dominant form of expressing the Jewish people's attempt to reach God. That is shown most clearly by the manner of celebrating the holiday of the covenant, **Shavuot**. He stress both the personal and communal aspects of that holiday. (38)

Eugene Borowitz is perhaps clearest in his emphasis on covenant and his stance on **halakhah** in the three volumes **Reform Judaism Today**, which provide the background for the "Centenary

Perspective" adopted by the Central Conference of American Rabbis in 1976. There he discusses both autonomy and the diversity in Reform Judaism as well as the extreme positions taken by Alvin Reines and Jakob Petuchowski. He avoids the traditional term **halakhah** as he feels that its use is often misleading because it creates a sense of authority which does not or should not exist. For him it is only a series of traditions of the past which may create ties with other Jewish groups but which are not authoritative. He feels feels that any other use of the term **halakhah** is "intellectually irresponsible and perhaps even deceitful."

Borowitz continues by stating that he is not sure how discipline can be reestablished in the group devoted to personal autonomy; he does not find **halakhah** compatible with Reform Judaism. That position is expressed equally clearly in his book. (39) As he views the Jewish world, he feels that volunteer observance by the individual is the only hope for our age. His criticism of some other movements within the Jewish community like the Conservative Judaism had already been anticipated by Mordecai Kaplan a generation earlier. His analysis of the extremes of Reform Judaism is equally critical and he does not find them acceptable either. So he returns to the existentialist covenantal position. "This approach does not restore Jewish law to us or the sense of discipline action connected with law. I do not see how we can do that theoretically or practically. Law and autonomy are incompatible as long as we are not in the days of the Messiah. We modern Jews, therefore, stand in a post-**halakhic** situation. This is one of the keystones of our liberalism. Yet it is important to overcome the anarchy which autonomous individualism can lead to in so pluralistic time as ours, since our covenant relationship to God is as a people, it implies some common way of Jewish living." (40) Actually Eugene Borowitz is not entirely sure that we are living in a post-**halakhic** world perhaps it is a pre-**halakhic** situation in which we found ourselves and "a day might come when a sufficient number of Jews trying to live in covenant come to do things in a sufficiently similar way that there customs begin significant for them and other Jews to take into account in determining their Jewish duty." (41) Borowitz's covenant is based upon the individual's commitment expressed more in a theoretical than in a practical **halakhic** manner.

As we turn to Emil Fackenheim (1916 -) we see a figure who was educated in Europe but has spent most of his adult life in North America and now resides in Israel. His philosophical works deal with post-Kantian issues and of course with the Holocaust. **Halakhah** plays a definite role in his Jewish thought. It is the response in the God-Israel relationship, "Moral law, mediated through the leap of faith, becomes the divine law to man. **Halakhah** is Jewish custom and ceremony mediated through the leap into Jewish faith; and it thereby becomes the divine law to Israel." (42) For him **halakhah** is the human response and in a sense Jewish gift to God. The laws have a potential of becoming divine. Fackenheim differentiates between law and commandment. For him the "law discloses only itself. A commandment discloses its giver along with itself. Obedience to a law does not necessarily create a relation to its giver. Obedience to a commandment necessarily creates such a relation. In Judaism revelation is commandment rather than law." (43)

The commandment presents a challenge to each individual Jew who through his free will can either accept or reject that challenge. Upon acceptance, that individual becomes a part of the Jewish people. For Fackenheim revelation is expressed through the commandment not through mysticism; it is the commandment which reveals the true pattern of Judaism. (44) As a liberal he sees the "**Torah** as the human reflection of a divine revelation, rather than itself literal revelation, the liberal can regard it as a human book which is the legitimate object of historical criticism, and whose commandments do not have, in letter, authority over him. But he may at the same time regard it as the prime means of access to a divine revelation which addresses him as much as his ancestors." (45)

These philosophical views of the **halakhah** are very much at variance with each other. They take us from the position of extreme autonomy to one of emphasis upon Jewish people. Some have dealt with the tradition in a semi-mystical view and others sociologically. Borowitz may be correct that the core problem lies in possessing no broadly accepted system of philosophy upon which we may agree as a basis.

It would be wrong to conclude this segment of my paper without a reference to the Winter issue of **Judaism** (1980) which was largely devoted to eighteen perspectives of Jewish law. Orthodox, Conservative, Reform, and Reconstructionist scholars reacted to a previously published paper by Robert Gordis. The points of view represented go from the totally static of J. David Bleich to non-**halakhic** stance of Alvin Reines. This effort toward broad discussion will be helpful for the future development of **halakhah**. Philosophy and theology have provided one avenue of approaching **halakhah**. The other has always been given through the practical responsa or codes. Let us now review that avenue.

The position of the **poseq** (decisor) has changed drastically within the Reform and Conservative movements during this century. In the Reform Movement for example despite the establishment of the Responsa Committee in 1907 no reponsa report appeared in the **Yearbooks** till 1911. The various chairmen who headed this committee in the early part of the century were faced by only a small number of questions which they felt required a formal answers. There may have been minor questions addressed to them as well but their number was probably rather small. The situation has changed during the tenure of Solomon B. Freehof and even more so during my tenure. The number of questions has vastly increased so that over one hundred questions are addressed to me each year; about half of them require a formal written responsum. In addition a score or more continue to come to Solomon B. Freehof.

Although in theory each chairmen of the Reform Responsa Committees have worked with their committee in practice that has not proven to be practical. Individual styles of the chairmen, the pressure of the work as well as the practical nature distributing a large volume of material for committee discussion has limited the affect of the committee. I have used it with those responsa of wider import and then incorporated suggestions into the responsa themselves whenever it seemed appropriate. However all the responsa of the Central Conference of American Rabbis have been written by the chairmen and essentially reflect the tendencies of the chairman.

The fact that responsa were written from a Reform background indicates that **halakhah** remains important despite the very different approaches taken by each rabbi. Autonomy versus discipline was the first question which each author had to decide. The former was given a secondary place.

Only Solomon B. Freehof among Reform respondents (1892 -) has done some extensive theoretical writing on the **halakhah** which may provide us with some insight into his stand on the **halakhah**. It is appropriate to review his thought as we honor him through this symposium. His introductions to volumes of Reform responsa and kindred works as well as various other essays indicate his position.

The introduction to **Reform Jewish Practice** (1944) present a picture of historic development and justification for change. Judaism has always been a religion with a different kind of relationship between deed and creed than expressed in Christianity. Solomon B. Freehof clearly indicates that the end of the introduction that the book is not intended to be a modern **Shulhan Arukh**. "It does not claim to lay down the norm of practice, except in two or three disputed situations where some preference must be made." (46) In that book as well as the second volume, Solomon B. Freehof presents the rabbinic background for numerous changes made by Reform Judaism. The two slim books intended to make the Reform Jew aware of "the great reservoir of Jewish law and custom preserved in the **halakhah**." (47) The author obviously felt that creative

halakhic application had a future.

In his book of **Reform Responsa**, the first of nine volumes of responsa, Solomon B. Freehof points out that the ethical idealism and the Biblical foundations of Reform Judaism could no longer be considered sufficient. There had been a cry for legal discipline. In an essay published in 1960 he analyzed Orthodox Judaism and the vast changes which have occurred not only in its expanding phase through the earlier centuries but also in the present age when massive segments of tradition are not longer observed. Most of its civil law and criminal law remains theoretical. As the entire system considers each segment of detail on the same plane as every other segment this is astonishing. Freehof has described this as following the Talmudic dictum: "As it is a duty to say what will be heard and obeyed so it is also a duty not to say what will not be heard and obeyed" (Yeb. 65b).

Freehof considered Conservative Judaism as an effort to meet the challenge of Orthodox non-observance. Conservatism "means to be rooted in the soil of history and to grow under the sun of legality." (48) However as Freehof points out there are problems connected with this as the task may prove too great and the bitterness of the Orthodox too difficult to overcome. Vast areas of Jewish law can simply not be reinterpreted in a manner applicable to the twentieth century and must be changed or abandoned.

Solomon B. Freehof sees Reform Jews as those who do not observe large areas of the law, but nevertheless consider themselves as religious individuals when part of the religious community. In this way they differ from other non-observant Jews as Reform Judaism grew in opposition to old line official rabbinic Judaism. Its pioneers were anti-rabbinical and so also rejected the rabbinic literature which was the source of traditional authority. This led to an emphasis on the Bible. However that soon proved insufficient as Biblical Judaism had no liturgy, no family rites and no fully developed pattern of life. The Bible always had to be interpreted within the framework of tradition. Furthermore, higher Biblical criticism also placed much of the Bible into a more human setting. Freehof therefore felt that we "must now grope toward a new definition of authority and revelation." (49) He repeatedly demonstrated that Reform Judaism in all of its manifestations has leaned heavily on the rabbinic past which of course involves **halakhic** literature. He has asked the usual questions about authority, the nature of our selectivity and the sense of obligation or lack of it felt among our people. For him "Reform response are not directive but advisory." (50) Furthermore they intend to be more liberal and affirmative than those of an Orthodox **poseq**.

In the second volume of responsa (**Recent Reform Responsa**, published in 1963, Solomon B. Freehof discussed some of the historical reasons for a renewed interest in **halakhah**. He felt that it lay partially in the expansion of the Reform Movement, the traditional roots of many of its members and the wish to establish some order in a chaotic situation. This has moved us away from excessive emphasis on the Bible and prophetic Judaism which did serve to establish the "centrality of religious morality." Yet rabbinic literature and **halakhah** must provide the practical expression for our ethical idealism. "We are increasingly aware that the totality of Judaism deserves the reverence our movement and all Jews." (51)

In **Current Reform Responsa**, published in 1969, Freehof the brief introduction emphasized that "we could not obtain our independence without denying and defying that (rabbinic) authority, but now we are strong and we can afford to be much more tolerant of the authoritative past." (52) Freehof here recognized various currents within the Reform Movement some of which have moved toward **halakhah** while others away from it. He pointed to various issues of conscience in which **halakhah** can not determine our course of action, for example, the rights of women which we have championed. In this introduction he stated that we will move toward a Reform code slowly as various **mitzvot** become accepted; he felt that the volumes of responsa were part of this process. "The **halakhic** literature is the grandest repository of Jewish thinking and feeling and what we may find in it as answer to the various questions which we ask may not, indeed, govern our lives but will at least serve us as a guide." (53) Freehof's fourth volume, **Modern Reform Responsa**, published in 1971, contained a largely historic introduction and then again dealt with the changes both sociological and religious which have affected tradtional Judaism as well its reaction to the Reform movement. He related the position of modern American responsa to the first vigorous **halakhic** attack on Reform Judaism presented by **Eleh Divrei Hab'rit** (1818).

In the volume, **Contemporary Reform Responsa** (1974) Solomon B. Freehof was primarily concerned with distinguishing Reform movement from

Orthodoxy. From an orthodox point of view the kind of choices that we continue to make about ritual are unacceptable, while from a Reform point of view, they lead to an attachment to tradition and a warmer feeling toward it. Basic distinction however remains as we do not accept the entire body of the commandment as divine. As Freehof analyzes what we accept, what is accepted and what is rejected, he pointed out that Reform has accepted a greater number of positive commandments which have a direct impact as well as negative commandments with a direct moral impact and most of all in **minhagim**. He felt in this way Reform had moved from an age dominated by philosophy to one in which psychology was the greatest importance. Our Reform reunion with **halakhah** reflects an appreciation for rabbinic literature as well as increased comradeship with the traditional community.

In **Responsa for our Time** (1977) Solomon B Freehof principally dealt with responsa as a source of history both for the incidental facts that they reveal about Jewish life and the mood of religiosity or neglect which they reveal. His accumulated volumes of Reform responsa provide the same kind of insight into our changing religious life in the middle of the twentieth century. The same theme is continued in his introduction to **New Reform Responsa** (1980) with its emphasis on Reform as a continually changing religion rather than one which remains eternally and everywhere the same.

The theme of **halakhic** neglect among traditional Jews has been expanded in a brief article in **Judaism** and into a small book which as yet unpublished. We can see from these introductions to the responsa volumes that Solomon B. Freehof developed an approach to **halakhah** as guidance not governance.

We should not be surprised that the other Reform scholars who have written responsa have avoided a philosophical rationale. Jacob Lauterbach and Jacob Mann were primarily historians, Israel Bettan's principle interest was **midrash** and homiletics. With the exception of Kaufman Kohler, first chairman of the Responsa Committee, philosophy and theology were not their major concerns. The responsa therefore were written from a practical and pragmatic point of view.

Outside the scope of this paper, but worth noting are the two guide books recently published by the Committee on Reform Jewish Practice. **The Gates of the Season** and **The Gates of Mitzvah** have made broad decisions on practice for the Reform movement. Some have been based on responsa, but the majority on the discussions and decisions of the committee. In a sense they have taken upon themselves the role of a **poseq**. As these are publications of the Central Conference, their role is different than Solomon Freehof's **Reform Jewish Practice**. The Volume, **Rabbinic Authority**, published by the Central Conference of American Rabbis has also set a different tone for **halakhic** discussions. The **Journal of Reform Judaism**, of course contains numerous essays on **halakhah**, but most of them are too brief for a sustained analysis. Since 1986 each issue has also included a responsum.

Conservative Judaism in Europe and during its early days in the United States produced n responsa and nothing that could be called a unified theory of **halakhah**. Zacharias Frankel devoted considerable energy to **halakhah**. His **Darkei Hamishnah** (1859) provided a historical foundation for the future study of **halakhah** in conjunction with various essays by him and others in the **Monatsschrift fuer Wissenschaft und Geschichte des Judenthums** (1851-1867) which he founded and edited. The rabbinic emphasis of Frankel became clear through the curriculum of the Jewish Theological Seminary in Breslau which he head from 1854 to his death in 1875. Half the courses dealt with rabbinics and almost entirely from a non-critical point of view during his tenure as director. Frankel set the tone for **halakhah** along with change, but he provided no clear criteria for such change.

The movement in Germany where it was part of the general liberal Jewish scene produced no responsa. In the United States the early energy of the movement was taken by its establishment and practical struggles with Orthodoxy, so nothing along these lines emerged.

As we turn to the later Conservative efforts in this direction we must immediately recognize the academic achievements of the scholars who have served the movement. Louis Ginsberg, Saul Lieberman, Boaz Cohen and Max Kadushin, among others have added to our understanding of the past. Their brilliance has been widely recognized. However, no consistent philosophy of Conservative **halakhah** has yet emerged. The volume **Conservative Judaism and Jewissh Law** (1977) makes this clear. Theoretical and practical issues have also been treated in **Conservative Judaism** and the **Proceedings of the Rabbinical Assembly**. The widespread concern and diversity of opinion is clearly evident. The differences between the right and left wing may restrain the movement from broad-------decision. We are somewhat limited by the reluctance of the Committe on Law and Standards to publish its responsa. Some have appeared in full in the **Proceedings of the Rabbinical Assembly** while only summaries of others have become available. The committee, established in 1927 has been served by a distinguished group of chairmen. The size of the committee has fluctuated; it has generally met at least several times a year and during special periods once a month. In the early days it functioned and was looked upon as a **Shulhan Arukh** committee, (55) sometimes subsequently it has been an instrument of change through **takanot**; on other occasions, this has not been considered its function. Prior to 1966 majority and minority opinions were issued with some regularity. This was done without the names of subscribing rabbis attached. The final decision then rested with the congregational rabbi. Unanimous decision are morally binding upon the entire movement. From 1966 to 1972 another system was tried and authorized responsa were issued with the names of members of the committee who were in agreement as signiatories. The system of majority and minority opinions was reinstated in 1972. The struggle between the right and left wings of the Conservative movement have been fought here as have the battles between the Seminary faculty and the leadership of the Rabbinical Assembly.

The Law and Standards Committee has issued some decisions without any written documentation. Responsa have also been written for the committee and remain in its files without any vote or action on them having been taken. By 1980, 20 responsa have been adopted unanimously; 30 have been adopted with a majority and a minority opinion. 79 additional responsa have been submitted in written form, but were not voted upon. 58 rabbis had participated by writing responsa; only a handful had written more than a few and most of them led to no action. Among them are Isaac Klein with 16, Ben Zion Bokser with 12, Aaron Blumenthal with 9, Philip Sigal with 8, and a few others with lesser numbers. This activity demonstrates a major interest in responsa, but also shows its limits. A glance at the subjects of the responsa shows that the majority have dealt with ritual matters and only 18 with broader concerns. These simple statistics which obviously need refinement, demonstrate that there is a major difference between concern over **halakhah** and the ability to react. It is possible that the majority of the Conservative rabbis make their own decisions locally and do not need to ask anyone for guidance; but judging from questions from Conservative colleagues which Solomon B. Freehof and I have received that is unlikely.

Concern over the **halakhah** is a regular theme of the **Conservative Judaism**; it has also been expressed in a broader format in **Judaism** which has been magnificently edited for many years by Robert Gordis. Various Conservative have written studies which contain sections on **halakhah**; they reflect the tensions and problems within the Conservative movement on this issue.

The leading practical **halakhic** authority of the American Conservative movement has been Isaac Klein whose book of responsa and his volume **a A Guide to Jewish Religious Practice** have formed a unified body of Conservative

halakhah. For Klein the **Torah** is divinely inspired; the **halakhah** has a central role in Jewish life; it can grow and is "not frozen". (56) Along with the traditional principles, Klein invokes history and sociology as part of the process of change, but "within Jewish law itself are principles that help it to grow and adjust." (57) Klein has rejected non-**halakhic** solutions to contemporary problems as well as new legislation which might adjust the system much more quickly. (58) He, for example, did not agree with the decision of the Committee on Law and Standards which permitted driving on **Shabbat**. (59)

It was more important for him that law possessed stability as only this provided the necessary authority. Isaac Klein made his decisions within this framework; only three of the fourteen responsa in his volume dealt with matters outside the realm of ritual. His volume **A Guide to Jewish Religious Practice** is a major effort to provide a code of practice for the Conservative movement in the area of religious ritual. The sources have been provided, customs along with some variations are noted, modern changes have been documented. It is thus a valuable work not only as a guide, but also as it marks where the movement stands at this moment. By publishing this work as an individual, the Conservative movement has chosen to take the traditional route of the previous historical codes.

Proper thoroughness would demand a lengthy discussion of the responsa and philosophical papers of David Novak, but as he is a participant in this symposium, let me be brief. His essays indicate a more traditional approach to Conservative Judaism. For him the **status quo** is normative and the burden of proof lies with those who wish to make changes. (61) Changes have taken place throughout our history, but our understanding of them must be from this point of view. The **halakhic** process is basic to him for Conservative Judaism irrespective of the differences which exist within the movement. (62) His two volumes **Law and Theology in Judaism** (1974 and 1976) contain numerous essays which are not quite responsa, but virtually follow the same path. They demonstrate great erudition and a willingness to operate within the framework which the author has set for himself. David Novaks' volume **The Image of the Non-Jew in Judaism**, An Historical and Constructive Study (1983) demonstrates this scholar's desire to deal with practical issues which lie beyond his earlier efforts. They can become the foundation for a new understanding of Jewish-Gentile relationships. This work provides the foundation for such a new approach.

David Novak's **first volume, Law and Theology in Judaism** (1974) presents a series of expanded responsa and thus a combination of practical and philosophical approach to modern **halakhah**. The thesis of this book is that "**halakhah** (law) and **agadah** (theology) are not only indispensable elements of Judaism in and of themselves, but that their interrelationship is equally important." In keeping with this thought, there is no general theoretical introduction, but theory and practice are tied together in the essays. Novak mentions his closeness to both Abraham Heschel and Boaz Cohen; he has been influenced by the latter's view of history and the former's theology. The questions which he has chosen for his responsa and the careful restrained answers presented indicate that change is possible, but should be made hesitantly. He would, for example, not eliminate the traditional statement "who has not made me a woman" from the liturgy, but advises a woman who finds it offensive not to read it. (63) In his answer to the question "May a Physician Perform a Circumcision?" Novak is guided ultimately entirely by the pragmatics of the situation. While in "Funerals in the Synagogue", he provides guidance without a directive.

David Novak's second volume with the same title also deals with the problem of **halakhah** and history; the latter must serve the former for the enterprise to remain Jewish. In his work Novak has dealt with the internal historic growth of **halakhah** as well as the historic external influences upon it. In his view "history (or theology) can **condition** a **halakhic** judgement. ... To use history as a ground for **halakhah** is to eliminate revelation as the trans-historical ground of the law. Without the grounding of revelation, **halakhah** loses its **ultimate** meaning. And to use theology as the immediate ground of a **halakhic** judgement is to deny **halakhah's** own **immediate** authority." (64) The responsa in the volume illustrate the same cautious approach whether dealing with women's rights, **kashrut**, or the priestly blessing. Novak criticizes the many Jews for whom "liberalism has replaced the **Torah** and Jewish tradition, and even reason, as the source of moral authority".

In his **Halakhah in a Theological Dimension** (1985), David Novak again deals with a variety of practical issues as for example "Women in the Rabbinate" and uses it to discuss a whole range of additional equalitarian issues which are bound to be raised. The basis of his thought is presented in the openning essay "Authoritative and

Changing." **Halakhah** is the normative principle for David Novak. "However, the authority of **halakhah** as a normative principle cannot be consistently maintained if the principle of change is elevated from a description to a prescription, as some traditionally inclined liberals would like to do." (65) "Thus, if **halakhah** is to remain law, the unchanging element must be primary and the changing element must be secondary to it." (66) If this is not so then either there is no authority for **halakhah** or its former authority is preempted by ethics. This, of course, leads to Judaism as primarily reacting to external sources. "Since Judaism is so elitist, particularistic and heteronomous, such ethical grounding of it clearly leads to the dismantling of almost everything in it which make Judaism unique. Much of Judaism cannot be justified on such ethical grounds, certainly not the **halakhic** system, as the example of Reform Judaism indicates." (67) Going in this direction leads to a hopeless effort to establish a system of Jewish ethics primarily on the **agadah**, which the **agadah** itself cannot sustain.

For Novak a historically oriented approach has become dominant. "The **halakhic** process stand between the revelation of Sinai and the full redemption of the days of the Messiah. The affirmation of revelation (an adequate theory of which is almost always absent from both fundamentalist and liberal rhetoric), as mediated by Jewish history, means that the **halakhah** is in substance the commandments of God as men and women attempt to fulfill them. Change then, is called for when the stastus quo prevents us from doing a **mitzvah** as fully and devotedly as we might. This often calls not only for new practical applications, but for new theories as well. ... The dynamics of recent history requite more than an acceptance of the past per se as automatically authoriatative. Faith must be more than antiquarianism. Revelation presents a source of authority which transcends the customary usage of any generation." (68)

As we review the world of the liberal **poseq** we can see that it remains strangely limited. The Conservative movement which should have a large responsa literature, must yet develop it. Thus far internal strife has prevented successful efforts along these lines. On the other hand responsa in the Reform movement have grown in importance and the movement as a whole has gone in this direction.

The **posqim** in neither of the liberal movements have more than a working philosophy, largely pragmatic in its orientation. There is general agreement on the importance of **halakhah** for modern Judaism. Its divine origin is not questioned nor is the historical process of change, but the nature of that change and how such changes are to be made in our time is very much debated. Furthermore there is also a great difference on the binding nature of the final decision. Seen from a philosophical point of view, these are major weaknesses, yet pragmatically the system seems to work and be in consonance with aspects of the rabbinic past. Even while we await a philosophical rationale, we continue to make decisions and perhaps that is the only way we can proceed.

Notes

1. Alexander Altmann, **Moses Mendelssohn** pp 381f; 486f.
2. W. Jacob ed., **The Pittsburgh Platform in Retrospect**, pp. 25ff.
3. Noah Rosenbloom, **Tradition in an Age of Reform**.
4. A. H. Friedlander, **Leo Baeck, Teacher of Theresienstadt**, p. 190.
5. Hillel Goldberg, The Early Buber in Jewish Law, **Tradition**, Spring, 1983, p. 66.
6. M. Buber, **The Eclipse of God**, p. 129 ff; **Moses**, p. 187 ff.
7. Maurice S. Friedman, "Revelation and Law in the Thought of Martin Buber," **Judaism**, V. 3, p. 14.
8. Martin Buber, **Moses**, p. 135.
9. Martin Buber, **Israel and the World**, p. 83.
10. "Martin Buber and the Law", **Journal of the Central Conference of American Rabbis**, April, 1971, p. 41.
11. Franz Rosenzweig, "The Builders: Concerning the Law," **Jewish Learning**, pp. 79 ff.
12. M. M. Glatzer on **Jewish Learning**, pp. 111, 119, 122.
13. Relation and the Law, **Ibid.**, p. 85.
14. F. Rosenzweig, **Kleinere Schriften**, pp. 109 ff, 120f.
15. "Toward an Understanding of **Halakhah,"Yearbook of the Central Conference of American Rabbis**, V. 63, pp. 686 ff.
16. **Conservative Judaism and Jewish Law**, p. 140.
17. **Ibid.**, p.141.
18. **Ibid.**, p. 143.
19. **Ibid.**, p. 147.
20. **God in Search of Man**, p. 344.
21. **Ibid.**, p. 274 f.
22. A. Heshel, **The Genesis of Faith**, p. 207.
23. **The Insecurity of Freedom**, p. 206.
24. **Understanding of Halakhah**, p. 150.
25. **God in Search of Man**, pp 328, 338; **The Insecurity**

26. **God in Search of Man**, p. 144.
27. **Judaism as a Civilization**, p. 433.
28. For an analysis see Richard Hirsh, "Mordecai Kaplan's Approach to Jewish Law," R. A. Brauner, ed., **Jewish Civilization: Essays and Studies**, Vol. II, pp. 155 ff.
29. M. Kaplan, **The Future of the American Jew**, p. 418.
30. "The Future of the American Jew" **Conservative Judaism and Jewish Law**, p. 17.
31. **Ibid.**, p. 22.
32. **Ibid.**, p. 25.
33. **Ibid.**, p. 18.
34. E. Borowitz, A **New Jewish Theology in the Making**. p. 206.
35. "Liberal Jewish Theology", **Yearbook, Central Conference of American Rabbis**, 1977, p. 139.
36. "Toward A Theology of Reform Jewish Practice", **Journal of The Central Conference of American Rabbis**. April, 1960, pp. 27 ff.
37. **Ibid.**, p. 30.
38. "On Celebrating Sinai", **Journal of the Central Conference of American Rabbis**, June, 1966, p. 112 ff
39. **Choices in Modern Jewish Thoughts - A Partisian Guide**, pp. 243 ff.
40. **Ibid.**, p. 243.
41. "Liberal Jewish Theology", **Yearbook, Central Conference of American Rabbis**, 1977, p. 167.
42. **Quest for Past and Future** - Essays in Jewish Theology, p. 110.
43. E. Fackenheim, "The Dilemma of Liberal Judaism", **Quest for Past and Future**, p. 143.
44. **Ibid.**, p. 145.
45. **Ibid.**, p. 146.
46. **Ibid.**, p. 15.
47. **Reform Jewish Practice** V .II, p. 7.
48. S. B. Freehof, **Reform Responsa**, p. 13.
49. **Ibid.**, p. 17.
50. **Ibid.**, p. 2.

51. **Recent Reform Responsa**, p. 11, also p. 2.
52. **Current Reform Responsa**, p. 3.
53. **Ibid.**, p. 7.
54. **Reform Judaism and the Legal Tradition**. The Tintner Memorial Lecture of the New York Association of Reform Rabbis.
55. **Proceedings of the Rabbinical Assembly of America** 1953, p. 66.
56. Isaac Klein, **Responsa and Halakhic Studies,** p. 128.
57. **Ibid.**, p. 130.
58. **Ibid.**, p. 134.
59. **Proceedings of the Rabbinical Assembly of America** 1950, pp. 177 ff.
60. **Judaism**, Winter, 1980, p. 40.
61. **Judaism**, Summer, 1977, p. 307.
62. **Ibid.**, p. 20.
63. **Law and Theology in Judaism**, Second Series, 1976, p xv.
64. **Ibid.**, p. 6.
65. **Ibid.**, p. 7.
66. **Ibid.**, p. 7.
67. **Ibid.**, p. 9f.

Chapter IV

Liberal **Halakhah**: Description, Appreciation and Critique

Eugene J. Lipman

Fifty-two years ago, when I arrived for my first appointment with Dr. Freehof, I came into this building for only the second time. The first was about 1932 for the Confirmation of my next door neighbor, Bernice Arnheim. Even while Dr. Freehof was becoming a major force in my life, Rodef Shalom remained merely the locale of his office, not more. But in 1940, my perception of this institution was radically changed by an incident.

I was asked to help with a young German refugee who had been refused admission to the Hebrew Union College. I inquired. The president said too many Germans had already been admitted; they had a doubtful future as rabbis in the United States. And, in addition, this young man had no money.

The first excuse is deliciously ironic, in view of the remarkable record of the Middle European immigrants, one of whom is the current president of our College Institute..

It was eventually agreed that the student would be admitted if fiscal support was forthcoming. Dr. Freehof waved his magic wand, the money came in promptly from Rodef Shalom, and the young man was admitted and ordained. He had a most useful career in the U. S. Military forces and in a major area of post-war Germany until his recent retirement. Rodef Shalom made in possible. Over the decades, this congregation has demonstrated its uniqueness as a caring, giving institution--routinely and on special occasions. Dr. Freehof acknowledged in several volumes of his responsa that the congregation had been instrumental in financing publication.

My last visit here was for the commemoration of the 100th anniversary of the Pittsburgh Platform - a significant experience for all of us who attended and for all who read the published papers. Thanks to the hospitality of Rodef Shalom, we were pushed to transcend our stereotyped and calcified views of the 1885 Platform. And now this opportunity, not only to say a slightly premature Happy Birthday to Dr. Freehof but, to use this Law Day once again to push our intellectual and spiritual frontiers a significant distance.

So I salute the people of Rodef Shalom who have accepted inspiration and direction from great rabbis, who have had the good sense to employ administrators of the caliber of Chester Bandman, **z"l,** and Vigdor Kavaler, and who have supported all manner of extraordinary occasions and causes generously and graciously.

Dr. Freehof was the first Reform rabbi who took a rightwing Conservative Jewish teenager and, forgive the word, converted me into a Reform Jew by choice. It all began with that first appointment with a somewhat younger but already awesome Solomon B. Freehof. I had just come to the conclusion, at age fifteen, that I could not go the Jewish Theological Seminary and I was rather lost. My late great uncle, Morris Neaman, suggested that I consult Dr. Freehof. He was accepting, non-judgmental. He wanted to see my report card from Allderdice each semester and later my transcripts from Pitt. He was willing to spend time studying with me and guiding my studies. He urged me to leave Pitt after my second year and get to Cincinnati before **g'dolei doro**, the great teachers of his generation left the scene. He signed my application for admission to our seminary.

Over the decades, Dr. Freehof has not always agreed with my career emphases. Some of you may know that his disagreements are couched as vigorously as everything else he says and writes. But he has always been available for correspondence and conversation, for answers to questions not only about Jewish law but about all manner of things. The paper I am about to read does not begin to express my gratitude to him. As one tiny symbolic evidence of my devotion, however, such Hebrew words as I shall utilize will be pronounced in the Ashkenazic form he uses exclusively.*

* * * *

Let me begin by looking at the words in the theme assigned to me by Rabbi Jacob. Our movement is called Liberal Judaism. It is also called Progressive Judaism, primarily in Israel. We in the United States tend to use the word Reform, and I am going to do so, in order to make clear that I do not include Reconstructionism, Humanistic Judaism or Conservative Judaism in what I have to say.

For the purpose of this paper, what is Reform Judaism? I faced two options: First,
Reform Judaism could be whatever Reform Jews believe or do as Jews - as individuals, as families,in our synagogues and in our national institutions.

* The printed text will use the same Sephardic transliteration as the other papers. (Editor)

Or, second, Reform Judaism could be what has been written by Reform Jews or adopted as policy by Reform institutions.

Because there are no competent contemporary data on the beliefs and actions of Reform Jews and our institutions, I decided to limit my inquiry to Reform literature - publications of the Central Conference of American Rabbis, works by individual Reform Jews on **halakhic** matters, which have appeared since the organization of the CCAR in 1889.

Our uses of the word **halakhah** are complex. Traditional **halakhah** is a corpus of law and the process by which the corpus is expanded. Both are believed by traditional Jews to have been revealed by God to Moses at Mt. Sinai - both the **Torah** text and the procedures for expanding on the text, ultimately to create more texts which assumed Divinely-revealed status. If we were required to use this definition, our symposium could not have taken place. Nothing I have read in the literature of our movement has postulated the doctrine that the words of the written **Torah**, the other two sections of the Hebrew Bible, the **Talmud**, or any other sacred text of Judaism was directly revealed by God to Moses at Mt. Sinai. Reform thinkers write of Revelation and of Mt. Sinai along a lengthy spectrum of convictions both positive and negative, but we have not taught or advocated **halakhah**, whatever we mean by it, as a Divinely revealed corpus or process.

We must inquire further before hazarding any definition of **halakhah** as the word appears in Reform literature and thought.

Among others, Rabbi Gunther Plaut has proposed that we not use the word **halakhah** at all within the Reform movement. For him, **halakhah** must be undergirded by the theological mandate: "you must." That is manifestly impossible within our movement as it currently functions. But, Plaut insisted, there has to be what he called an "operative ought." He went on:

We must begin with where we are as Jews. We begin where our people are in our congregations. We begin with **minhag**.....We start with what we do traditionally and then make it freely into something that we decide is our must, our ought, our **mitzvah**. The rabbi's task is to lead people from minhag to **mitzvah**." (1)

Rabbi Martin Rosenberg denied that Reform had ever broken its deep ties to the **halakhah**. Today, he wrote, we must expand our adherence to traditional modes without losing our fundamental Reform principles:

"Reform Jews must believe that the authenticity of our religious conduct may be determined by what we understand traditionally as the mandate by God to walk in holiness, and by how we implement in our lives those traditional values believed to be rooted in a higher cosmic order. The **halakhah** of our fathers has a rightful claim upon us, if only by its durability. But Reform **halakhah** must be willing to listen to the mandates of our own modern world as well. What becomes **halakhah** for us must ultimately be determined by the living consensus of the covenanted community of Reform." Rosenberg then called for undefined sacrifices on the part of Reform Jews to preserve the unity of the Jewish people. That was in 1973. (2)

Twenty years earlier, Rabbi Eugene Mihaly had posited the thesis that there can be no Judaism without **halakhah**, defined almost exactly as Plaut had done: the **must**. He was prepared to rely on the knowledge, the devotion and the confidence of the individual rabbi to "apply the divine imperatives of historic **halakhah** to our life situation." (3)

Several of our colleagues have suggested both general characteristics of our approach to **halakhah** and how we should undertake to make our **halakhic** decisions.

My predecessor at the UAHC, Rabbi Jacob D. Schwarz, noted four discrete categories of practice among us:

1. Cases where a practice is not **halakhically** prohibited and we approve it: for example, **qaddish** for twelve months, not eleven months minus one day; the right of a non-Jew to handle the **Torah** during our services.

2. Cases in which we have discarded the **halakhic** practice: for example, in mourning customs, in officiating at marriages during the **omer** season, our denial of special status to **kohanim** and **levi-im**.

3. Cases in which we have modified **halakhic** practice: for example, our shorter **Torah** reading, or is some congregations our adoption of the triennial reading cycle; our non-observance of the second day of the **r'galim** the pilgrimage festivals.

4. Cases in which we uphold **halakhic** tradition: for example, not officiating at intermarriages, prohibition of weddings on **shabbat**, maintenance of the traditional categories of consanguinity. (4)

Rabbi Stephen Passamaneck, our **landsmann** and Dr. Freehof's student, characterized our relationship with the **halakhah** in part as follows:

a. Reform Judaism has always functioned within the juristic frame of reference which has characterized much of Jewish thought.

b. Reform has differed from Orthodoxy over what may be described as a theory of law. Our working theory involved the freedom to make an informed choice, the persuasive guidance of rabbinic tradition, the ethical and moral standards of Jewish life, and in part of the concept of progressive revelation. (5)

Rabbi Jakob Petuchowski published his **Heirs of the Pharisees** in 1970. In it, he proposed these criteria for determining Reform practice (he did not use the word **halakhah**):

1. What has been the main direction of the Tradition?

2. How can I best realize the traditional teaching in my life and in my life and in my situation?

3. How do I hear clearly the voice of my conscience?

4. How do I express my feeling of responsibility toward the covenant community? (6)

These four concentrate on the individual. Petuchowski went on to be concerned about the **qahal qadosh**, the holy community--the individual congregation, a **havurah**, etc. Then he expressed concern for the whole household of Israel, and like Dr. Freehof some years earlier, pleaded for negotiations to try to reach understanding about matters of **ishut**, personal status.

The most systematic single work done within our movement which might be called **halakhic** is the brief book **A Guide for Reform Jews**, originally written by the late Rabbi Fred Doppelt and our colleague Rabbi David Polish, revised by Rabbi

Polish in 1973. Doppelt and Polish, too, posited the need for "musts" in Reform Jewish life. They called them **mitzvot**. **Halakhot** are the detailed procedures for carrying out the **mitzvot** Then there are **minhagim**, customs which may well vary from individual to individual and congregation to congregation. (7)

If I may interject a subjective note here, it seems to me that, gradually, we are concentrating constructively now on the concept of the life of **mitzvah**, and the search for the **mitzvot** we are under command to perform. I find this even truer among the colleagues with whom I meet and with serious lay people than I do reflected in the language of our responsa, though certainly the word **mitzvah** is used more frequently and more confidently in our time than it was in the earlier decades of American Reform.

In that earlier literature, the words **mitzvah** and **halakhah** were rarely mentioned. Isaac M. Wise talked of the **Talmud** and sometimes of talmudic law. Several other circumlocutions turned up in the early literature, but not often. It is noteworthy that, before 1906, the papers and committee reports in CCAR meetings on matters involving Jewish law were relatively infrequent. In general, the members of the Conference tended to accept the statements of the so-called French Sanhedrin of 1807 and of the synods of German Reform. The overwhelming interest of the pioneer members of the CCAR was Prophetic Judaism, its theological underpinnings and its universalistic implications. These themes dominated the sermons of the rabbis in their congregations, their speeches at the meetings of the CCAR, and their writings.

From time to time, within the CCAR a committee studied some issue, and reported with recommendations. There was full discussion at an annual meeting and a vote which became the CCAR position, non-binding, of course. (Occasionally, on major issues like intermarriage and patrilineality, this is still so, but in general our pattern has clearly changed.

In 1891, Schlessinger read a detailed paper on cremation in Jewish law. He concluded in favor of approving it. Two years later, Felsenthal presented an equally detailed paper challenging Schlessinger both on details and in his conclusion. Burial is a **mitzvah** - that word appears, which was unusual then - and cremation is not. But, no matter what his views, the rabbi must officiate and give a eulogy at a cremation service. The CCAR voted:

"Be it resolved that in case we should be invited to officiate as ministers of religion at the cremation of a departed co-religionist we ought not to refuse on the plea that cremation is anti-Jewish or irreligious." (8) That is still our formal position, reaffirmed by the Responsa Committee in 1980.

In 1892, Wise chaired a committee on the circumcision of adult converts. His committee "proved" that "no introductory rites were canon law." The definition of "canon law" was **Torah** or **Mishnah**. Since these rites for adults came later than the second century C. E. they were **minhag** only. The resolution which passed:

"That the Central Conference of American Rabbis....considers it lawful and proper for any officiating rabbi, assisted by no less than two associates, to accept into the sacred covenant of Israel and declare fully affiliated to the congregation (**dover shebiqdushah**) any honorable and intelligent person, who desires such affiliation, without any initiatory rite, or observance, whatever."

The convert was to declare willingness:

1. To worship the One, Sole, and Eternal God, and none besides Him;
2. To be conscientiously governed in his or her doings and omissions in life by God's laws ordained for the child and image of the Maker and Father of all, the sanctified son or daughter of the divine command;
3. To adhere in life and death, actively and faithfully, to the sacred cause and mission of Israel, as marked out in Holy Writ. (9)

In 1895, Rabbi Wise asked a committee to consider this question: "Is Post-Biblical and Patristic Literature religious authority for American Judaism? Putting aside the quaint verbiage, this is clearly a core question. The committee reported three principles:

1. Religious literature is of great value.
2. Each generation has added a "wing to this great treasure-house."
3. We, too, must do so, "as the spirit of our time directs." The climax of the report:

" To have awakened the consciousness of this historic fact is the great merit of Reform Judaism; and the more this consciousness grows upon our mind, the more the conditions and environments of our modern life force it upon us, the more persistently we have to assert:
(italics theirs) that our relations in all religious matters are in no way authoritatively and finally determined by any portion of our post-Biblical and Patristic literature." Please note the deliberate exemption of the Bible from that stricture.

Despite the clear general decision, exceptions cropped up in decision-making. For example, in 1914, in a responsum about who should stand during **Qaddish**, Kaufmann Kohler wrote:

"If this question refers to the preceding, I would suggest that the mourners stand at all recitals of the **Qaddish** for the dead for whom mourning is a legal duty. If this question is general, I refer to **Yoreh Deah**, Hilkhot Avelut, where certain distinctions are set forth at the established **din and minhag**" (emphasis mine). (10)

The number and scope of questions and responses gradually increased, especially after 1911. Kohler was involved, as sole respondent, in tandem with Neumark, or in one case with Lauterbach, in twenty-one **teshuvot**. Two of them involved only date, not a point of view.

A new tone came into the expressions of Reform teachers regarding **halakhic** matters during the period dominated by Dr. Jacob Z. Lauterbach. His rabbinic knowledge was prodigious and he poured it into his twenty-one responsa, many of which were lengthy documents. His conclusions tended to be carefully written expressions of continuing ties with traditional practices, to be modified when either contemporary Orthodox practice did not take all traditional opinions into proper account or a change essential in our time. Let me cite a few:

Should non-Jewish workmen be permitted to do construction work on the synagogue building on **shabbat**? Lauterbach made a persuasive case that such work by an independent contractor did not essentially violate Sabbath law. But the possibility of giving the appearance of a synagogue employee or agent so occupied would be against **halakhah**.

Lauterbach concluded that the synagogue should not permit work on the Sabbath even if it costs extra money "I make this decision with great hesitancy because my sentiments are against giving the permission but I must, in truth, state that the law does not offer any serious objection to it." (11)

Lauterbach's responsum on worshipping with covered or bared head is a classic of rabbinic detail. He stated that the almost universal practice in recent centuries of covering the head is "merely a matter of social propriety and decorum." His conclusion, in the realities of our time, sounds romantically naive: "We should realize that this matter is but a detail of custom and should not cause arguments between Orthodox and Reform. It is a detail that is not worth fighting about. It should not separate Jew from Jew and not be made the cause of breaking up Jewish groups or dividing Jewish congregation." (12)

At the request of the Board of Governors of HUC, the ordination of women was discussed by the CCAR in 1922. Lauterbach's responsum was relatively brief, since the rabbinic material was sparse and all on one side. Should we adhere to the **halakhic** prohibition? His answer, strongly stated, was positive. His reasons for upholding the prohibition were a combination of tradition thinking and personal bias:

1. We might jeopardize our own ordination.
2. There is no shortage of rabbis which required the addition of women.
3. Women would not raise the standard of the rabbinate. On the contrary they would lower if because they would be split between the full devotion our profession requires and the duties of motherhood and homemaking.
4. The subordinate position of a woman

rabbi's husband would have a deleterious effect on congregational families.

5. There are other avenues open to women for religious and educational work.

6. The only reason to ordain women is to be consistent about our commitment to full equality. But consistency is not the main characteristic of rabbis. (13)

I believe Lauterbach's greatest responsum was on Birth Control. It was a pioneering work, thoroughly researched and cogently presented. His conclusions flowed directly from the rabbinic material. He recognized continuing differences of opinion within the contemporary Orthodox rabbinate. We need not seek unanimity, he wrote, only "to have good and reliable authority for our decision, even though other authorities may differ. We have the right to judge for ourselves which view is the sounder and which authorities are more current." (14)

The literature makes it clear that our evolving relationship with **halakhah** did not move mono-directionally or in a straight line. The work of Israel Bettan is evidence of this fact. Dr. Bettan wrote twenty-three responsa. In none of them did he include any detailed biblical or rabbinic citations. His responsa are brief. The longest, on euthanasia, is less than three printed pages in length Most are a page or less. Many of Bettan's opinions are subjective to the borderline of caprice. Here are several:

A question had to do with the presence of national flags in the synagogue, an old custom. The sole source of Bettan's answer was U. S. Army regulations, though there is rabbinic material and though the standard source of protocol on this matter is a State Department regulation. Bettan encouraged the presence of the American flag as conductive to worship. He objected to the presence of the Israel flag, unless an Israeli high official is in the synagogue or it is a notable anniversary. (15) Incidentally, in 1977 Rabbi Jacob and the Responsa Committee offered no objection to either flag. They suggested that the flags might be flown in the foyer of the synagogue, not in the synagogue proper. (16) Dr. Bettan was asked about the marriage of a **kohen** to a divorcee, prohibited in traditional **halakhah**. He selected some rabbinic material which denigrated the antecedents of the **kohen**, since no records of the **qehunah** have been kept since the fifth century C.E. He concluded:

"

When, therefore, Reform Judaism chose to ignore the nominal distinction betwen the ordinary Israelite and the **kohen** - a distinction which has persisted to this very day - it did not so much depart from tradition as it did display the resolute will to surrender a notion the validity of which eminent rabbinic authorities had repeatedly called in question." (17)

When Bettan was asked about an impending marriage between a Negro man, preparing for conversion, and a white Jewish woman, he found no intrinsic objection. But if the woman's family objections persisted, the rabbi should arrange for another rabbi to officiate. And if the civil law objected on anti-miscegenation grounds, the law was to be obeyed. This was in 1954. (18)

Without comment, let me proceed to Dr. Freehof's tremendous output. In the collection entitled, **American Reform Responsa**, edited by Rabbi Jacob, thirty-five of 173 Responsa were written by Dr. Freehof. In his nine volumes of Responsa published by our College-Institute there are 419 responsa on 101 different subjects. Small wonder that rabbinical thesis and doctoral dissertations are being written to scrutinize and analyze this huge collection. I shall do neither. I shall describe a few samples which may indicate some the major pillars on which Dr. Freehof has stood as decisor and where he fits into the approaches of Reform leaders to **halakhah**..

Dr. Freehof has always emphasized the influence of Dr. Lauterbach on his thinking and on the methods he has utilized in responding to **halakhic** questions. But it must also be said that he is very independent in his use of traditional texts, in his invoking of other contemporary factors, and especially in the great importance he attaches to the mood of the people in our congregations. Dr. Freehof is a firm believer in collective mood, and in our obligation to lead our people only in directions in which they are prepared to be led. There is clear rabbinic precedent for this attitude. Rabbis Shimon b. Gamliel and Eliezer bar Zadok said: "We make no decree upon the community unless the majority are able to abide by it (**Avodah Zarah** 36a). The majority requirement does not appear in a similar statement in **Tosefa** Sota (15:10). Here is one example of its use by Dr. Freehof:

He was the third Reform authority to write on the question of blowing the **shofar** in the Reform synagogue when **Rosh Hashanah** falls on the Sabbath. Basically there is no difference among them, since it is clear that blowing the instrument is not the problem in traditional **halakhah** but carrying it or repairing it would be, and none of the Reform authorities worried about those details. Freehof's **hiddush**, his new insight, reads as follows:

"We should also consider the mood of

our people, since these matters count a great deal with us. It is, of course, illogical that some of our people should object to the sounding of the **shofar** on New Year Sabbath. They certainly do not object to the playing of the organ, which is at least as violative of Sabbath laws Still, some people might think that since it is both Sabbath and New Year they would rather not have the **shofar** blown. If the rabbi senses there is that much feeling against it, he should not permit the blowing of the **shofar** on the New Year Sabbath." (19)

In 1965, a Reform rabbi was asked to officiate at the marriage of a Karaite woman Dr. Freehof's response concentrated on the problem of the divorce practice of the Karaites, which caused rabbinic suspicion of **mamzerus**, from a later marriage whose offspring might not be able to marry any Jew except another **mamzer**, not a bastard as we use the term, but a child of a forbidden relationship. Freehof's conclusion is of interest:

"Beyond all this, there is a special consideration involved in the fact that we are Reform Jews. We accept the validity of civil divorce, at least in the United States. (This has been the position of the CCAR since its beginnings, though not all Reform rabbis conform to it.) The reason for refusing a Karaite certainly does not have validity for Reformers. If we accepted the old grounds for refusal, we could not marry a considerable percentage of people we do marry. Since the authorities agree that Karaite marriages are valid and Karaites are of Jewish descent, and since the only objection is the validity of their divorce and the consequences drawn from it, we should have no hesitation in officiating at the marriage of a Karaite and a

Jew." (20)

One of Dr. Freehof's most famous responses was written in 1958, when the connection became known between German measles in pregnant women and deformities in the fetuses they were carrying. May such a woman terminate pregnancy through abortion? Both classical and contemporary **halakhic** authorities were cited by Dr. Freehof in his responsum. He dealt with the circumstances in which abortions were permitted or prohibited back into Talmudic times, and with disagreements among several later and contemporary authorities. The hub of the matter is the degree and form of damage to the mother from continuing the pregnancy to term. The strictest authority I know, whose work postdates this responsum, is Rabbi J. David Bleich of New York, who would permit abortion only to save the physical life of the mother. Dr. Freehof came down with a broader permission. He wrote:

"....Since there is strong preponderance of medical opinion that the child will be born imperfect physically and even mentally, then for the mother's sake (i.e., her mental anguish now and in the future) she may sacrifice this part of herself. This decision thus follows the opinion of Jacob Emden (18th century) and BenZion Uziel (20th century Israel, Sephardic Chief Rabbi) against the earlier (17th century) opinion of Yair Chaim Bachrach." (21)

By the way, this is one of the few responsa in Reform history which served as the basis for institutional resolutions of position not only by the CCAR but by the UAHC and the National Federation of Temple Sisterhoods as well.

In 1977, Dr. Freehof retired as chair of the Responsa Committee, became its honorary chair, and was succeeded by Walter Jacob. The New York office did not even have to change the committee's address:

There has been no lessening of the interest of Reform rabbis and lay people in the field. On the contrary, in these ten years, Rabbi Jacob and members of his committee have published seventy responsa. In addition, Rabbi Jacob has issued two hundred eighteen as sole author. The idea that individual members of the Responsa Committee should sign on to specific **teshuvot** with Rabbi Jacob is new and of interest. It spreads responsibility for the editing and consideration of the work and may give additional cachet to the material.

Rabbi Jacob and his committee undertook a full-scale review of all extant responsa. Some were updated with footnotes. Others were clarified. Still others were rewritten fully. Let me cite two examples:

First, on **bar and bat mitzvah**, along with their relationship to Confirmation. The review consisted of a description of the historic evolution of all three practices both in traditional **halakhah** and within Reform Judaism and led to the following brief conclusion:

"We encourage the celebration of the **bar/bat mitzvah** at the age of thirteen as an initial step toward maturity. The ceremony must lead to continued Jewish education, Confirmation, and high school graduation. The mood of that day should be religious and festive, so that the child and the parents feel a sense of **mitzvah**." (22) It has a stable feel.

A question asked by a lay person in 1982 gave the committee an opportunity to review the question of a rabbi officiating at a marriage between a Jew and a non-Jew. The committee did not repeat the **halakhic** data contained in earlier responsa; it cited them. It noted the 1973 decision of the CCAR, then gave fifteen reasons for our contemporary position. In view of the pressures on us to officiate at intermarriages, I suspect these arguments are most helpful to colleagues. (23)

In many ways, the serious writing of Reform leaders over the decades about the role **halakhah** should play and may play in Reform Jewish life has significantly raised our consciousness about approaches to and relationships with **halakhah** both as corpus and as process. No rabbi can and no lay person should avoid the profound implications of these books, essays, and articles for our life as Jews. For this work we should be grateful.

L'maaseh in functional terms, the hundreds of responsa written by Reform scholars have significantly raised our consciousness about the possibilities for enhancing our lives as Jews by coming closer to the traditions of our people. For this we should be grateful.

In reality, the theoretical and functional writings of our scholars and teachers have done much to restore to Reform Jews and to Reform Judaism the centrality of **mitzvot** as the operative answer for us to the core question we must ask as children of the covenant people. I believe our authenticity as a Jewish movement is so much clearer now. What does God require of us? **Mitzvot**; for this we should be profoundly grateful." (24)

More than incidently, this body of writing has given to Reform Jews and their teachers a fine and joyous opportunity to learn and to teach. It is great intellectual fun to teach a course with **American Reform Responsa** as the text. I derive pleasure from discovering in numbers of congregational bulletins that this kind of adult education is increasing among us each year.

And thus far we have accomplished what we have accomplished without spiritual civil war and without giving up our autonomy and our pluralism. Forty one years ago Dr. Freehof wrote: "We have achieved order and we have achieved it in liberty." (25) From my perspective forty years later, I would say: We have achieved a measure of order and we have achieved it in liberty.

The question has been asked many times: have we too little order among us and too much liberty? Before I conclude with my response to that question, let me raise a few relatively specific areas in which I feel our writings and positions place us in a peculiar posture. They are in no particular rank order:

1. It has been stated often that individual informed conscience must be a major consideration for us. But informed or not, conscience is unreliable. It is too easy to rationalize for convenience, comfort, advantage, especially for rabbis. To pinpoint our most poignant current example: we all know that rabbis are under severe pressure to officiate at intermarriages and that, despite the Placement Commission rules, increasing numbers of congregations will not elect a rabbi unless he or she does. I have listened to some depressingly ingenious statements by young colleagues trying desperately not to give in on a

matter of conscience and yet obtain employment.

2. The same caution can be expressed regarding sociological and psychological factors when an individual is making an **halakhic** decision or even when the Responsa Committee is doing so. The tendency toward subjectivity is real and the possibilities of selecting among data are great. Rabbi Emanuel Rackman, now president emeritus of Bar Ilan University, wrote well of both the values and dangers in such data, from his modern Orthodox perspective, in a fine article. (26)

3. In that article, Rabbi Rackman raised another issue for us. He urged the Orthodox rabbinate to become teleological - to ask about the purpose of the specific **halakhot**. He mentioned four issues which, in his view, could be solved by such an approach: **mamzerut**, interest-taking, organ transplants, and the status of the occupied territories; i.e., the distinction between **kibbush ha-aretz** - conquest of the Land - and war. Our need is very similar.

4. The same volume includes a good article by Rabbi Theodore Friedman on Conservative Judaism and **halakhah**. It is a source of pain to me that our responsa literature makes no use of some of the fine work done by the Committee on Law and Standards of the Rabbinical Assembly, our differences notwithstanding.

5. Our colleague Lou Silberman, formerly professor at Vanderbilt University contributed the Reform perspective in that trio of papers. One of his concerns was the manner in which we in Reform have utilized the rabbinic concept of **dina d'malkhuta dina**, literally the law of the kingdom is the law, first expressed by Samuel, a third-century Babylonian luminary.

The so-called French Sanhedrin of 1807 had attempted to please Napoleon and ensure French citizenship for Jews by declaring carefully a distinction between Jewish religious matters, which are eternal, and political views which ceased to be operative when a Jewish state ceased to exist. They deduced that religious marriage and divorce, for example, required prior civil authorization. The CCAR went further, declaring that civil divorce was sufficient and no Jewish act or document was required. With out exception, **halakhic** authorities, past and present, have carefully and specifically denied to the secular state the right to determine Jewish practice in matters of ishus, of personal status.

The late Sephardic Chief Rabbi of Israel was asked if a man, having been married only civilly, could then be married Jewishly in a secular state which prohibits polygamy. He ruled that, even though the first marriage is not valid Jewishly, a **bet din** cannot help him break the civil law he accepted in his first marriage.

In the literature about **dina d'malkhuta dina**, there is much about the use of civil contracts and official documents. It has been ruled almost without exception that a civil document like a death certificate or deposition can be used to prevent a woman from becoming an **Agunah**, chained to a missing husband, unable to marry again.

Beyond these two, I have been unable to find any rabbinic support for extending the concept of **dina d'malkhuta dina** into matters of **ishut**. (27) I stress this issue because of its importance in our relationships with other Jewish religious movements in our day.

6. It is also a source of pain to me that we have not used rabbinic sources and tests in our social justice pronouncements. We have correctly accused ourselves of "**pasukism.**" We write an ethical position paper and begin it or end it with a **pasuk**, a verse from the Bible. That puts a kosher stamp on it. I contrast this procedure with the brilliant responsum written by the Orthodox Massachusetts **bet din** supporting the boycott of California lettuce and grapes ten years ago during the first battle of the Farm Workers Union. A good rabbinic principle, **oshek**, oppression, was their platform. As Professor Passamaneck reminds us, (28) there is a lot or relevant **halakhic** material available to us for this primal purpose - if we wish to discover it.

7. Finally, I suspect we sometimes overstate the effectiveness of our work among rabbis and especially lay people. Statistics on the number of questions asked do not necessarily correlate with what rabbis and congregations do or care about. For some, I fear, this is an intellectual game, rather like Talmudic **aggadah**-serious but not operative.

I have a dream. In my dream Rabbi Jacob and his committee continue to receive many questions and inquiries. They respond to the factual inquiries much as they have been doing. **she-elot**, however, are approached in this way:

1. Is there a deep-seated reason for us to diverge from traditional **halakhah** in connection with this question?
2. If there is, we undertake a full exposition of the traditional texts with representation of all sides, and with serious concern for our pattern of practice within Reform. If the committee is unanimous, the **teshuvah** can

be issued as we currently do.
3. If there is disagreement within the committee on the position we should take, both majority and minority reports should be submitted in writing to the membership of the CCAR for formal debate and decision, as has been done with a few major matters like intermarriage and patrilineal descent.

The first is the most important to me: Is there a deep-seated reason for us to diverge from traditional **halakhah** in connection with this question? I am among those, probably a minority of CCAR members, committed to attempting to build some sense of structure among us and even some discipline which can have a measure of consistency and coherence, not only in the area of **ishus**, as Dr. Freehof urged almost a generation ago and which is still debated among us, but in our entire approach to what we do as a movement. I have seriously done so personally for a long time, and worked hard at the undertaking in my congregation.

I believe deeply that Kaufmann Kohler was correct when he wrote:

> "I am the very last to propose a new book of laws, but I insist that there be a clearer system and certain guiding principles in the practice of the modern rabbi." (29)

Notes

1. **Yearbook, Central Conference of American Rabbis,** V. XC, pp. 64-5.
2. **Ibid.**, V. LXXXIII, pp. 150-151.
3. **Ibid.**, V. LXIV, pp. 214-226.
4. **Reform Judaism**, HUC Press, 1949, pp. 227ff.
5. Reform and **Halakhah**: The State of the Art,

HUC-JIR 1967, pp. 14-15.
6. Jakob Petuchowski, **Heirs of the Pharisees**, pp. 174-179.
7. **Yearbook, Central Conference of American Rabbis,** V. III, p. 347.
8. **Ibid.**, V. III, p. 94f.
9 **Ibid.**, V. XXIV, p. 153.
10. **Ibid.**, V. XXXVII, p. 206.
11. **Ibid.**, V. XXXVIII, p. 603.
12. **Ibid.**, V. XXXII, p. 156ff.
13. **Ibid.**, V. XXXVII, p. 384.
14. **Ibid.**, V. LXIV, pp. 79-80.
15. W. Jacob, ed., **American Reform Responsa**, pp. 67f.
16. **Yearbook, Central Conference of American Rabbis,** V. LIII, p. 86.
17. **Ibid.**, V. LXIV pp. 77f.
18. S. B. Freehof, **Recent Reform Responsa**, p. 40.
19. **Yearbook, Central Conference of American Rabbis,** V. LXXV, p. 98.
20. **Ibid.**, V. LXVIII, p. 122.
21. W. Jacob, ed. **American Reform Responsa**, pp. 86-9.
22. **Yearbook, Central Conference of American Rabbis,** V. XCII, pp. 213-215.
23. **Ibid.**, V. XCII, pp. 21-29.
24. **Ibid.**, V. LIV, p. 292.
25. **Yearbook, Encyclopedia Judaica,** 175-76, pp. 12 ff.
26. S. Shilo, **Dina D'malkhuta Dina**, Hebrew University Press, 1975.
27. S. Passemaneck, **Motion for Discovery**, Louis Caplan Lecture, HUC-JIR.
28. **Yearbook,** Vol. XVI, p. 60 **Central Conference of American Rabbis.**

Chapter V

Liberal **HALAKHAH** - A Conservative Approach

David Novak

1. Introduction.

At the very outset, I must confess that the title of my talk today, "Liberal **Halakhah** - A Conservative Approach", was assigned to me; I did not choose it. Nevertheless, I do not protest in that I find it rather challenging for it could have several meanings. In a logical sense, the terms "liberal" and "conservative" seem to be mutually exclusive - **satrai ahadadai** as the **Talmud** would say, or **contradictio in adjectu** as the logicians would say. If so, then how can there a be "a conservative approach" to "liberal **halakhah**"? However, perhaps something more is implied in the title which should be explicated for the sake of clarity - **hasurai mehsara** as the **Talmud** would say, or providing the excluded middle as the logicians would say. Perhaps, whoever entitled my talk really meant, "Liberal **Halakhah** - A Conservative Approach As Distinguished from A Reform Approach". In other words, it might be assumed that there is such a thing as "Liberal **Halakhah**", or better, "Liberal Judaism" - as in the title of the symposium itself - and that there are two approaches to it, namely, Reform and Conservative.

Now I know that there are some Conservative Jews, especially some Conservative rabbis, who would readily accept such an assumption. (1) However, I am not one of them. Indeed, in reviewing my last book on **halakhah** a prominent Reform Rabbi, Dow Marmur of Toronto, wrote, "It ggis difficult to discern the difference between this position and the stance of normative Orthodoxy in contemporary Judaism." (2) Frankly, I would probably be more comfortable at a symposium where my talk would be entitled, "Traditional **Halakhah** - A Conservative Approach As Distinguished from An Orthodox Approach." But, alas, it is a sad comment on the xenophobia rampant in the Orthodox world today that it is most unlikely that any such symposium would ever take place - at least in public. Hence, to this symposium on Liberal Judaism I come as an outsider, albeit a friendly one for I would not want to miss an opportunity to talk with any serious group of Jews who are concerned with **Torah**, especially with its **halakhah**

Furthermore, not only do I not find Liberal Judaism an appropriate common term to be assumed in our discourse, I do not find "Liberal **halakhah**" appropriate either. For if one is to distinguish liberal **halakhah** from Conservative **halakhah** - taking these terms in their original denotation - I suppose one would then assume that "liberals" are more lenient (**meqilim**) and "conservatives" are stricter (**mahmirim**) as such adjectives are used in popular discourse about **halakhah**. And, of course, it would be easy to show how I have been stricter on a number of **halakhic** questions where our celebrated guest of honor, Dr. Freehof, has been more lenient. (3) This is true, but it is not essential. No intelligent and honest **halakhist** is lenient for the sake of leniency or strict for the sake of strictness. Rather, one is to have worked out a unified point of view - a **sheetah** as the **Talmud** would say - and from that unified point of view certain conclusions are to follow as corollaries from a principle. At this level, strictness and leniency are not the issue. Thus, as the **Mishnah** puts it in several places, **nimtza humro qulo**, namely, the same unified principle which led one to a stricter conclusion on one question leads one to a more lenient conclusion on another question, and both conclusions are so necessarily. (4) There is only contradiction in the minds of the unlearned (**amei ha-retz**). They only see **halakhists** as being either laissez-faire or fanatical. In the minds of the learned (**talmidei hakhamim**), on the other hand, there is no contradiction because they understand the principle as the transcending middle term prior to both of the concluding disjuncts. Thus in a famous passage in the **Tosefta** we read:

> Whoever wants to be strict with himself and follow both the strict opinions of the School of Shammai and the School of Hillel, about him Scripture states, "and the fool (**ha-kesil**) walks in darkness" (Ecclesiastes 2:14). Whoever grabs the lenient opinions of the School of Shammai and the School of Hillel, he is wicked (**rasha**). Rather, if one wants to follow the opinions of the School of Shammai, let him do so whether they are lenient or strict; likewise with those of the School of Hillel. (5)

Clearly, then, only learning provides a sound middle ground between foolishness and wickedness. That it is why it is even prior to practice in importance. (6) Moreover, the disputes between these two schools and the anymosity they entailed are attributed by some to their lack of proper education in the sources and practical experience in applying them. (7)

In fact, even in those areas of **halakhah** where strictness and leniency are taken to be primary terms, there was growing impatience with this conceptual state of affairs. (8) Thus, one of the greatest medieval **halakhists**, R. Solomon ibn Adret of Barcelona, in writing about the **Talmud's** prescription that the view of one early authority (**tanna**) is to be followed on a certain issue whether it is strict or lenient, states, "it is not because of strictness or leniency but because it follows from a principle (**debemilta talva**) . . . one point does not contradict the other; there is a reason (**taama**)." (9)

It is only when we are unclear about the **halakhah** that strictness (**humra**) and leniency (**qula**) are decisive terms, such as in the well-known principle, "when in doubt (**safeq**) about a Scriptural law, follow the stricter option; when in doubt about a rabbinic law, follow the more lenient option." (10)

It is at the level of a rationally justifiable principle, which for Talmudists is the optimal foundation of a practical approach in Judaism, where our discourse should take place - should take place, but rarely does. That is why I am so happy to be here with you today, for it is such a rare opportunity to enage in truly rational discourse about **halakhah**, discourse which cuts across the usual political lines in Jewry and where none of us needs - or should be allowed - to engage in the meaningless political posturing or the equally meaningless ecumenical niceties which pass for rational discourse in our Jewish community. In this sense, I come here today to respectfully analyze an aspect of current liberal **halakhah** with which I very much disagree, namely, the so-called "Patrilineal Decision". Although I do not recall that Dr. Freehof has explicitly dealt with this question, I infer from what he has written on related questions that he is in favor of it; **l'av be-fairus itmar ela me-khlala itmar** as the **Talmud** would say. (11) Thus, I have come here today to dispute with him and with his disciples, and I hope that this will be adispute which will surely be for the sake of God (**le'shem shamayim**) who is Truth. (12) Indeed, may it be said of me here today, **amicus Freehofi, amicior veritati**: I love Freehof, but I love truth even more, precisely because neither he nor I nor any of you possesses it, but all of us seek it. Thus, let our affection and respect for Dr. Freehof's work be the beginning of our quest, and let truth be its end. (13)

2. **Halakhah** and Theology.

Few issues have so stirred contemporary Jewish passions as the question of "who is a Jew?" (**mi hu yehudi**), and more specifically of late, the decision of the Reform community to allow Jewish identity to be presumed by either matrilineal or patrilineal descent. Heretofore, this decision has been debated on either practical or theoretical grounds. On practical grounds, it has been argued by proponents of the decision that sociological realities should take precedence over traditional rules. On theoretical grounds, it has been argued by proponents of the decision that individual conviction should take precedence over the mere accident of birth. (14) However, most of the practical debate has not been **halakhic** in any strict sense, and most of the theoretical debate has not been theological in any strict sense. And none of it to my knowledge has been in the context of the correlation of **halakhah** and theology.

It is in the context of the correlation of **halakhah** and theology where discussion of the truly normative question of **what-is-to-be** should take place. Furthermore, the one prescribing **what-is-to-be-done** must be part of the community to whom this prescription is being addressed; indeed, he or she must be at its very cutting edge to have any credibility at all in this domain, which is essentially a moral enterprise. (15) Thus, the assertions of both **halakhah** and theology here are made as claims to be heard by the religious community committed to the truth the **halakhist** or the theologian is purporting to proclaim and expound. And, in questions of major Jewish concern, the **halakhist** must also be a theologian and the theologian a **halakhist**. (16)

This might be better understood if one looks upon living Judaism as a normative field, containing a practical/**halakkhic** pole at the one end and a theoretical/theological pole at the other end. Here we might look to **Talmud Bavli**, not only for data (of which it is the prime source for both **halakhah** and theology),
but also for method. How does **Talmud Bavli** relate the two poles of the normative field? It does so by asking one of two fundamental questions, which one to be asked depending on where the problem requiring inquiry is situated. If the problem is that two different practices are being advocated by two different authorities, then the question is **be-mi qa-mipalgei**, that is, "what difference in theory lies in the background?." (17) Conversely, if the problem is that two different authorities have advocated two different theories, then the question is **mi banihu**, that is, "what practical difference results from this theoretical distinction?." (18)

3. The **Halakhah** of Patrilineality.

The Reform decision on patrilineality - which is a legal ruling and, therefore, **halakhic** in the broadest sense of that term - makes two innovative points. (1) Having a Jewish mother or a Jewish father alone only creates a presumption of Jewish identity. That presumption can only be validated by a subsequent pattern of life which includes publically recognized affirmations of

Judaism. (2) That being the case, no formal conversion to Judaism is required of these persons for them to be considered full Jews in the Reform community. From these two explicit points, one can draw the following two corollaries. (a) Persons having two Jewish parents are considered full Jews **ab initio** even if they do not subsequently lead a recognizably Jewish religious life. (b) Persons having no Jewish parents must have a formal conversion to Judaism if they are to be considered Jews at all. Finally, as a general conclusion, calling these innovations "patrilineality" is a misnomer, for "patrilineality" is only one aspect of the innovative ruling and it is certainly not the type of patrilineality which most likely obtained in the biblical period. (19)

The two corollaries just drawn are valid inferences if one simply looks at the two innovations in the immediately practical sense of **halakhah le-ma-aseh** Moreover, they are valid inferences if one employs sociological criteria, namely, there are an increasing number of Jewish men married to non-Jewish women and many of these men consider their children to be members of the Jewish people. (20) However, if one looks for the theoretical background of these two innovative points, both corollaries are questionable in their very logic. Taken together these two innovations seem to be based on two assumptions. (1) Jewishness is ultimately determined by the free choice of the individual to be part of a religious community. (2) This choice is made manifest by living a life that is recognizably Jewish in the religious sense, that is, it is a process rather than something created by the single event of a conversion ceremony. In other words, the choice is one made through a process of tacit agreement. (21) And, it is not too difficult to see how consistent these assumptions are with the basically democratic theory of citizenship accepted in those Western societies where Reform Judaism has flourished. (22) Finally, this theory also seems to imply that one can also choose to renounce what might be called his or her "potential" Jewish identity from birth.

Now if these two assumptions are seen as the theoretical background of these two practical innovations, neither of the two corollaries drawn from the practical innovations is in truth defensible. For if Judaism is essentially a matter of free will, a freedom which manifests itself in a publically discernable way of life, then it should not make any real difference whether one has two Jewish parents, only a male Jewish parent, only a female Jewish parent, or no Jewish parents at all. One does not choose his or her parents, but it would seem that underlying the Reform **halakhic** ruling is the basic premise that one indeed does choose whether to be a Jew or not to be a Jew, and that decision is foundational for determining one's Jewish (or non-Jewish) identity. In other words, still adhering to what are essentially three different Jewish statuses (namely, those having two Jewish parents, those having only one Jewish parent, and those having no Jewish parents at all) is not logically consistent once the theory behind the practice is adequately uncovered.

Uncovering this basic assumption shows that Reform Judaism has made a fundamental switch in the whole question of determining Jewish identity. Heretofore, one's Jewish identity was determined either by ascertaining whether one was born to a Jewish mother or by ascertaining that one was properly converted (albeit certain details of what comprises "proper" conversion are the subject of **halakhic** debate, even in the classical sources. (23) However, here we have a basic theoretical contradiction, a contradiction which leads us right into theology. For if Jewishness is a matter of birth, then conversion as an act of volition should be inadmissable. And, on the other hand, if Jewishness is a matter of volition, then birth should be irrelevant; everyone should be required to convert to Judaism. Nevertheless, despite the fact that there are some **aggadic** texts which do compare the whole Jewish people, especially at the Sinai covenant, to converts (24) the **halakhah** regards birth as being the primary criterion of Jewishness and conversion very much secondary to it. In fact, one way of expressing irony in **Tamud Bavli** with the phrase, "the native born is on earth and the convert in heaven?!" (**yatziva b'ara ve-giyora bishmei shamaya**). (25)

In order that the secondary reality of conversion be consistent with the primary reality of Jewish birth, **Talmud Bavli** constructs a **fictio juris** by declaring that "one who converts is like a newborn child" (**ger shenitgayer keqatan shenolad dami**). (26)

In fact, one kabbalistic theologian saw converts to Judaism as being in truth Jewish souls who were accidentally born into gentile bodies, and conversion for them is the restoration of the metaphysical **status quo ante**. (27) Furthermore, the convert does not become Jewish simply because of his or her own personal decision. Rather, the prospective convert presents himself or herself before a Jewish court (**bet din**) three Jewish judges decide, based on social and political criteria over and above the apparent religious sincerity of the conversion candidate, whether or not to accept him or her into the Jewish people and, hence, whether or not to conduct the rites of conversion for this person. (28) Following this basic logic, certain **halakhic** authorities accepted the conversion of infants even without their subsequent explicit consent or rejection when they reached adulthood. (29) Thus, we see that the primary criterion of birth forces conversion to be interpreted as something far more complex than a strictly personal decision of an autonomous individual to become a Jew. (30)

4. The Theology of Jewish Identity.

We have now moved from a practical ruling to the legal theory behind it. But, we can and we must probe more deeply and when we do, we will move into the area of theology proper. For the deeper debate between Traditional Judaism's insistence on matrilineality as the primary determinant of one's Jewishness (and this would even be so if one believed that true patrilineality obtained in the biblical period) and Reform Judaism's adoption of a basically (although not yet fully) voluntaristic determinant -- the deeper debate is about the theological doctrine of the election of Israel (**behirat yisrael**). The authentic theological question here is: Did God choose the Jews, or did the Jews choose God?

Clearly, the whole tendency of classical Jewish theology: biblical, rabbinic, kabbalistic, is that God chose the Jews, and that that choice was initially without their consent, even withtheir actual resistance. (31) A seminal **aggadah** colorfully stated that God suspended Mount Sinai over the heads of the people of Israel and said to them that if they did not accept His **Torah**, He would bury them under the mountain right there and then. (32) This theology lies behind the **halakhic** ruling that no matter what a Jew does, even if he or she converts to another religion, that person remains a Jew - albeit a bad one or a very bad one and one who can be denied virtually all of the privileges of the Jewish religious community. (33) Now this does not mean that Judaism could survive much less flourish if the Jews had not subsequently decided to accept the **Torah** willingly. But, the key point in this theological doctrine is that the covenantal obligation is not grounded in that acceptance; that acceptance only confirms (and develops) what has already been given. That is why in classical rabbinic parlance "revelation" is **matan torah**. (34)

Now that we are fully within the realm of theology, we can see that revelation and the election of Israel are two sides of the same theological coin. And, both sides of this theological coin presuppose the doctrine of creation. Usually, one thinks of creation as being Judaism's most universalistic doctrine and the election of Israel as being its most particularistic doctrine. However, that assumption always leads to the universal/ particular antinomy, a perennial item on the agenda of modern Jewish thought - an antinomy that no amount of Hegelian type dialectics can adequately overcome. One should, rather, look at the problem as Yehezkel Kaufmann did when he asserted that these two doctrines are essentially correlated. Only a God who freely created the entire universe has the prespective and the freedom to choose one people for a special covenantal relationship. (35) The gods of the pagan nations did not choose them, but rather both were correlated by a natural necessity. Both lived and died in tandem. And, it is precisely because God freely chose to create the universe **ex nihilo** that such claims as "shall the judge of the whole earth not do justice?" (Genesis 18:25) can be cogently made. Likewise, it is precisely because God freely chose to create Israel as His own treasure people (**am segulah**) that such claims as "remember Abraham, Isaac and Israel your servants, to whom You yourself promised and said to them, 'I will increase your progeny like the stars of the heavens'" (Exodus 32:13) can be cogently made. In other words, in creation God wills all the possibilities and in the covenant God chooses one of them. God is, therefore, responsible for His own choices. (36) Hence, in practical terms, this is why in basic questions of Jewish identity - both individually and collectively - the will of the Jews is deemphasized (but not eliminated lest the covenant turn into a Calvinistic type predestination) in order to emphasize all the more strongly the primacy of the will of God. There is voluntarism here to be sure, but it is divine not human. God chose the Jews.

5. The Liberal Theology of Autonomy.

The Reform departure from the traditional **halakhic** criterion of matrilineality is not, then, simply a return to another corollary of the divine election of Israel, that is, patrilineality, as we have seen. It is based, rather, on the primacy of human choice or autonomy. Thus, Professor Manfred Vogel, in a closely reasoned theological defense of the Reform decision, recently wrote:

"Indeed, one suspects that in all likelihood some of the supporters of this resolution may well have intended for the resolution to make such an implication, namely, to imply that Judaism is purely a community of faith completely devoid of any involvement with the ethnic-national dimension. Still, the number of such people today can not be too high. Rather, one would suspect that many more people, while fully accepting the involvement of the ethnic-national dimension with the constitution of Judaism, are nonetheless very uncomfortable with having their Jewishness determined exclusively by the event of birth and consequently would want to interpret the latter stipulation in the vein suggested above so as to add more religious, spiritual criteria to the determination of one's Jewishness." (37)

The important thing to note about this theological statement is that "religious" and "spiritual" criteria are voluntaristic, whereas "ethnic-national" criteria are not. Clearly the former are more humanly compelling than the latter. Nevertheless, the correlation of these two aspects of Jewishness does not seem to function in the original unity we saw in the correlation of election and conversion in Traditional Judaism. For election covers both nonvolitional Judaism - what Dr. Joseph B. Soloveitchik calls **b'rit goral** ("the covenant of fate") -- and voluntary responsive Judaism -- what he calls **b'rit vi-ud** ("the covenant of faith." (38) For could one not say that the election of the native-born Jew is the direct result of his or her birth, whereas the election of the convert is his or her hearing of the divine call and then being accepted and thus reborn into the Jewish people?

The Reform position, conversely, struggles with the antinomy of nature and freedom precisely because human freedom -- in this case the freedom to chose God and thereby compose a **Torah** (and within it an **halakhah**) out of that choice -- is not just confirmational for the Reform, but it is foundational. This is why it seems to me, Reform theologians (as recently as Eugene B. Borowitz), have always been so concerned with the question of autonomy. (39) This would also explain why Reform theologians have always been so concerned with the most liberal possible attitude towards the acceptance, if not the actual proselytization, of gentile converts to Judaism. (40) All of this is completely consistent with the voluntaristic tendency discussed above.

6. Conclusion.

We have seen how probing the theoretical background of this dispute of practical **halakhah** leads to a distinction in legal theory and, ultimately, to a fundamental cleavage in theology. In fact, the seriousness of this current debate can only be grasped if seen from both the practical and the theoretical poles of what I have called the normative Jewish field. For if only seen as a practical debate, the issue seems too mundane for such passion; and if only seen as a theoretical debate, the issue seems too abstract for such passion. As a traditional Jew, one who accepts the **full** authority of the traditional **halakhah**, I cannot accept the new Reform **halakhah** on this issue and on other issues as well. Here I stand with Zechariah Frankel, who had the same problem with Reform over a century ago. And, on the theological level, I cannot accept liberal notions of the primacy of religious autonomy. I could not accept them long before the patrilineal decision was made. The decision, therefore, did not surprise me. It followed a definite historical trend, albeit not yet to its logical conclusion. Since that logical conclusion has not yet been reached, there is still time for me to ask my Reform brothers and sisters the following question. Even if you as Liberal Jews follow the famous liberal dictum of Mordecai Kaplan that "the ancient authorities are entitled to a vote -- but not to a veto," (41) do you really believe you have enough votes in the sources of Jewish law and Jewish theology to make such a radical innovation and thus depart from traditional Jewish practice on **the** fundamental question of Jewish identity?

Notes

Parts of this paper were originally read at a session on Constructive Jewish Theology at the Annual Meeting of the Association of Jewish Studies on December 15, 1986 in Boston. I thank those who commented on my remarks then and thus helped me to very much revise them for this paper.

All translations are by the author.

1. See, e.g., Jacob B. Agus, "The Nature and Task of Liberal Judaism", **Dialogue and Tradition**, New York, 1971, p. 567, where he writes, "the Reform and Conservative movements should work together as bearers of Jewish liberalism," p. 567.

2. Review of **Halakhah in a Theological Dimension** Chico, California, 1985, in Religious Studies and Theology, 6, p. 1-2, Jan., May, 1986, p. 93. See, also, Lawrence J. Kaplan, "The Dilemma of Conservative Judaism", **Commentary**, 62. p. 5, Nov., 1976, p. 46, for much the same judgment by an Orthodox rabbi.

3. E.g., see "Women Called to the Torah", **Reform Responsa**, Cincinnati, 1960, pp. 40-42; cf. D. Novak, **Law and Theology in Judaism,** New York, 1976, 2: pp. 144-145 and "Aliyot for Women" in **Tomeikh Kehalakhah: Responsa of the Panel of Halakhic Inquiry**, Mt. Vernon, NY: Union for Traditional Conservative Judaism, 1986, pp. 23-31. See **Recent Reform Responsa**, Cincinnati, 1963), chap. 34, "Cohen Marrying Daughter of a Mixed Marriage", pp. 162; cf. D. Novak, "Review-Essay" Isaac Klein, **Responsa and Halakhic Studies, Judaism**, 25. pp. 4 (Fall, 1976), pp. 500-501. See Freehof, **Op. Cit.** chap. 41 ("Abortion"), pp. 188-193 and **Reform Responsa for Our Time**, Cincinnati, 1977, chap. 55 ("Abortion and Live Fetus Study"), pp. 256-259; cf. D. Novak, **Law and Theology in Judaism**, New York, 1974, 1: pp. 114-124. See **Modern Reform Responsa**, Cincinnati, 1971, chap. 35 ("Allowing A

Terminal Patient to Die"), pp. 198-203; cf. D. Novak, "What is Euthanasia According to Jewish Law?" (Heb.), **Hadoar**, 55. 5, Dec. 5, 1975, pp. 73-74 and **Law and Theology in Judaism**, 2 pp. 98

108. All of these comparisons are on questions where Dr. Freehof has confined himself to traditional **halakhic** sources and has not based himself on Reform departures from those sources.

4. See **M**. Hallah 4.5; **M**. Sanhedrin 11.2; **M**. Parah 4.4

5. **T**. Sukkah 2.3, ed. Lieberman, 262 and parallels. Also, Bet Shammai were not uniformly strict or were Bet Hillel uniformly lenient. See **T**. Eduyot 2.3

6. See **Sifre**: D'varim, no. 41, ed. Finkelstein, pp. 85-86 and parallels.

7. See **T**. Sotah 14.9, ed. Lieberman, pp. 237-238 and parallels.

8. E.g., for the growing impatience with the conceptual inadequacy of **qal vehomer** type inference by later **Amoraim**, see **B**. Berakhot 23b and **B**. Qiddushin 4b.

9. Note on **B**. Eruvin 46a. See **Ibid**., 7a; also, **B**. Yevamot 88a and note of R. Yom Tov ben Abraham Ishbili (Ritba) thereon.

10. **B**. Betzah 3b. The same applies to the **halakhic** principle that one is to follow the stricter option when the **Talmud** presents two contradictory inferences and they are "left standing" (**teiqu**) because we are unsure what principle is primary. See R. Isaac Lampronti, **Pahad Yitzhaq**, s.v. "**teiqu**"; also, Louis Jacobs, **Teiku - The Unsolved Problem in the Babylonian Talmud**, London and New York 1981, pp. 302-307.

11. See **B**. Berakhot 9a and parallels. I infer this from Dr. Freehof's earlier acceptance of the 1947 resolution of the C.C.A.R. which was the main Reform precedent for this recent decision. See "Who is a Jew?", **Recent Reform Responsa**, chap. 14, pp. 75-76.

12. See M. Avot 5.17 and B. Shabbat 55a and parallels.
13. See M. Eduyot, end.
14. For the ruling and some of the discussion it occasioned, see **Judaism**, 34 p. 1 (Winter, 1985).
15. See Jacques Maritain, **Existence and the Existent**, trans. L. Galantiere and G. B. Phelan (Garden City, NY, 1957), 61, n. 3; R. M. Hare, **Freedom and Reason** (Oxford, 1963), 73;

Paul Tillich, **Systematic Theology** (Chicago, 1951), 1, pp.10-11;

Paul Ricoeur, **History and Truth**, trans. C. Kebeley (Evanston, IL, 1965), p. 179.
16. See Novak, **Halakhah in a Theological Dimension** chap. 9.
17. See, e.g., **B**. Kiddushin 47a-b; also, E. E. Urbach, **Halakhah: Meqororoteyha Ve-hitpatehutah** 123ff.
18. See, e.g., **B**. Baba Metzia 15b-16a.
19. For an analysis of the **halakhah** of matrilineality, see Wayne R. Allen, "Statement on Patrilineal Descent" in **Tomeikh Kehalakhah**, 59-60. For an historical analysis of this question, see Shaye J. D. Cohen, "The Origins of the Matrilineal Principle", **AJS Review**, 10, p. 1, Spring, 1985, pp. 13ff.
20. See Alexander M. Schindler, "Facing the Realities of Intermarriage", **Judaism**, 34, p. 1, Winter, 1985, pp. 85ff.
21. Re tacit agreement, see Plato, **Crito**, 50Bff.
22. See John Rawls, **A Theory of Justice**, Cambridge, MA, 1971, pp. 541ff.
23. See, e.g., **B**. Yevamot 45b and **Tos**., s.v. "**mi**". For a full discussion of this whole question, see D. Novak, "The Legal Question of Converts of Questionable Status", **The Jewish Law Annual** (forthcoming).
24. See, e.g., **Pesiqta de-Rav Kahana**, 12, ed. Mandelbaum, 1, p. 216;

Tanhuma: Yitro, ed. Buber. 2:38a. Cf. Keritot

9a where converts are compared to Israel, but not vice-versa.

25. **B**. Yoma 47a and parallels.

26. **B.** Yevamot 22a and parallels. For a good contemporary exposition of the theology in the background of this **halakhic** ruling, see Michael Wyschogrod, **The Body of Faith**: **Judaism As Corporeal Election**, Minneapolis, 1983, pp. 175ff.; also, his "Love Your (gentile) Neighbor", **Sh'ma**, 9/175, May 1979, pp. 113-114.

27. R. Judah Loewe (Maharal of Prague), **Tiferet Yisrael**, Intro.- See B. L. Sherwin, **Mystical Theology and Social Disent**: **The Life and Works of Judah Loewe of Prague,** Oxford, 1982, pp. 102-106. See **B**. Shabbat 146a.

28. See **B**. Yevamot 24b; also, **B**. Kiddushin 70b and parallels; and W. G. Braude, **Jewish Proselytizing in the First Five Centuries of the Common Era**, Providence, RI, 1940, p. 42ff.

29. See Maimonides, **Hilkhot Avadim**, 8.20 and R. Abraham de Boten, **Lehem Mishneh** thereon; **Hilkhot Isurei Bi'ah** 13.7; **Hilkhot Melakhim**, 10.3 and R. Joseph Karo, **Kesef Mishneh** thereon. Maimonides' view seems to be based on **J**. Yevamot 8.1/8d re **M**. Makhshirin 2.7. Also, see Rabbenu Nissim (Ran) on Alfasi: **Ketubot**, ed. Vilna, 4a. Cf. **B.** Ketubot 11a and commentators thereon.

30. See, esp., **B**. Yevamot 47a re Deut. 1, p.16., also **B**. Qiddushin 62a, b. Note, also, that **B**. Yevamot 22a and parallels speak about the convert "being converted" (**she-niegayyer**) not about himself or herself "converting" (**she-mitgayer**). As in all legal texts, the grammar is important.

31. See Novak, **Halakhah in a Theological Dimension**, 116ff.; also, **Law and Theology in Judaism**, 2, p. 18ff.

32. **B**. Shabbat 88a.

33. **B**. Sanhedrin 44a re Josh. 7:11; **J**. Demai 2.4; **Rosh:** Baba Metzia, chap. 5, no. 52. Cf. Abrabanel on Deut.: Nitzavim, ad q. 14.

34. See M. Kadushin, **The Rabbinic Mind**, New York, 1952, pp. 57-58.
35. See **The Religion of Israel**, trans. M. Greenberg, Chicago, 1960, pp. 127-128, 163-164; also, Novak, **Halakhah in a Theological Dimension** pp. 64-65.
36. See Novak, **Op.Cit.**, pp. 124ff.
37. "The Resolution on Patrilineal Descent: A Theological Defense", **Modern Judaism**, May, 1986, pp. 131.
38. See "**Qol Dodi Dofeq**" in **Divei Hagut Vehe Arakhah** Jerusalem, 1982, pp. 32ff.
39. See his "The Autonomous Jewish Self", **Modern Judaism**, Feb., 1984, pp. 39ff.
40. See Hermann Cohen, **Religion of Reason Out of the Sources of Judaism**, trans. S. Kaplan, New York, 1972, 283; Kaufmann Kohler, **Jewish Theology**, Cincinnati, 1918, 411ff.; Leo Baeck, **The Essence of Judaism**, trans. V. Grubenwieser and L. Pearl New York, 1948, pp. 77-80, pp. 257-260. Also, see two monographs by two Reform rabbis, which provide historical material for this basic thesis: B. J. Bamberger, **Proselytism in the Talmudic Period**, Cincinnati, 1939; Braude, **Jewish Proselytizing**, etc. (see **supra**, n. 28). For a critique of this whole approach, see D. Novak, "Should Jews Proselytize?", **Sh'ma**, 9/179, Oct. 19, 1979, pp. 153-155.
41. **Not So Random Thoughts**, New York, 1966, 263. I thank Rabbi Richard Hirsch of the Reconstructionist Rabbinical College for locating this quote for me. Actually, it is in all likelihood based on G. K. Chesterton, **Orthodoxy**, Garden City, NY, 1959, pp. 47-48.

Contributors

Peter J. Haas - PhD from Brown University in Judaism in Late Antiquity with a specialty in Ethics. He teaches at Vanderbilt University in Nashville. He has published a number of books and articles in Jewish law, responsa and Jewish ethics.

Walter Jacob - Rabbi of the Rodef Shalom Congregation, Pittsburgh, Pennsylvania. Chairman, Responsa Committee of the Central Conference of American Rabbis. The author or editor of twelve books and more than seven hundred published articles and sermons.

Eugene J. Lipman - President of the Central Conference of American Rabbis and Rabbi Emeritus of Temple Sinai, Washington, D. C. The author and editor of four books as well as studies and essays.

David Novak - Rabbi of Congregation Darchay Noam in Far Rockaway, New York and Adjunct Professor of Philosophy at Baruch College of the City University of New York. He is the author of a number of studies in Jewish Law, ethics and theology.

Jakob J. Petuchowski - The Sol and Arlene Bronstein Professor of Judaeo-Christian Studies and Research Professor of Jewish Theology and Liturgy at Hebrew Union College-Jewish Institute of Religion in Cincinnati, the author or editor of over thirty books and more than six hundred published articles.